Academic Advising
in the Community College

Academic Advising in the Community College

Edited by Terry U. O'Banion

ROWMAN & LITTLEFIELD
Lanham • Boulder • New York • London

Published by Rowman & Littlefield
An imprint of The Rowman & Littlefield Publishing Group, Inc.
4501 Forbes Boulevard, Suite 200, Lanham, Maryland 20706
www.rowman.com

Unit A, Whitacre Mews, 26-34 Stannary Street, London SE11 4AB

Copyright © 2020 by Terry U. O'Banion

All rights reserved. No part of this book may be reproduced in any form or by any electronic or mechanical means, including information storage and retrieval systems, without written permission from the publisher, except by a reviewer who may quote passages in a review.

British Library Cataloguing in Publication Information Available

Library of Congress Control Number:2019951027
ISBN 978-1-4758-5084-0 (cloth)
ISBN 978-1-4758-5085-7 (paper)
ISBN 978-1-4758-5086-4 (electronic)

Contents

Foreword   vii
     Walter G. Bumphus

Preface   ix
     Terry U. O'Banion

1. An Academic Advising Model for the Twenty-First Century   1
    Terry U. O'Banion

2. The Power of Advising in Community Colleges   13
    Evelyn Waiwaiole and Courtney Adkins

3. A Framework for Advising Reform   31
    Serena Klempin, Hoori Santikian Kalmakarian, Lauren Pellegrino, and Elisabeth A. Barnett

4. LifeMap 2.0: The Evolution of a Developmental Advising Model at Valencia College   55
    Ed Holmes, Evelyn Lora-Santos, John Britt, and Kathleen Plinske

5. Flight of the Hawks: A Pathways Approach to Advising   75
    Sheryl Otto and Victoria Atkinson

6. Building Pathways to Student Success at the Community College of Baltimore County: The Role of Academic Advisement in Guided Pathways   101
    Nicole Baird and Jennifer Kilbourne

7. Establishing a Culture of Completion through Advising at West Kentucky Community College   117
    Renea Akin and Octavia Lawrence

About the Contributors   139

About the Editor   145

Foreword

Walter G. Bumphus

The growing focus on college completion among policy makers, academicians, and leading foundations has also brought renewed examination of the elements that foster student success. In his recently published work, *Completing College: Rethinking Institutional Action*, Vincent Tinto, considered the preeminent scholar on student retention, identifies four crucial "conditions" that promote student success and thus lead to higher completions. Those conditions are expectations, support, assessment and feedback, and involvement.

Related to assessment, Tinto writes, "Students are more likely to succeed in institutions that assess their performance and provide frequent feedback in ways that enable students, faculty, and staff alike to adjust their behaviors to better promote student success." I couldn't agree more. The first eighteen years of my thirty-year career in higher education were spent as a dean of students and then vice president of student affairs. I have seen personally the need for, importance of, and outcomes from having a consistent and well-planned advising program. Believe me, there is no more humbling experience than knowing that the guidance you provide a student will, to a significant degree, help to determine how well that student succeeds on campus, and ultimately in the world of work.

Thus, I could not have been more enthusiastic to see another preeminent scholar, Terry O'Banion, who pioneered one of the early models in student advising at community colleges, take up that mantle once again with this current work. The author has done so with a passion uniquely his own and with an intellect that has led innovation for decades.

I can speak to Terry's earlier work firsthand. First at East Arkansas Community College and then at Howard Community College in the late 1970s and early 1980s, I used the original O'Banion Model of academic advising to implement what I found to be highly effective advising programs. It provided the appropriate student-centered approach, one that I believe was a precursor for today's expanded focus on student success. The validity of that approach and the heightened need for solid, structured, and sequential academic advising is just as relevant today. When I speak with my daughter, Fran Maynard, who serves as North Lake (Texas) College's Dean of Student Success and has responsibility for academic advising there, she underscores the fundamental importance of this need.

At state and national levels, recognition of the importance of better student supports and integrated advising programs is clear. California is currently moving forward with the Student Success Act, which requires that campuses participate in a common assessment system and post a student success campus score as a condition of funding. The final report of the 21st Century Commission on the Future of Community Colleges, sponsored by the American Association of Community Colleges, included multiple recommendations that address the importance of increasing the numbers of students completing certificates and degrees through better student support and aligning courses of study to workplace requirements.

Academic Advising in the Community College provides contemporary analysis of four successful advising models at community colleges today and two special insight papers from leaders at the Community College Research Center and the Center for Community College Student Engagement, along with O'Banion's updated article, "An Academic Advising Model for the 21st Century." Originally published in 1972 in the *Junior College Journal*, O'Banion's model has been adapted by hundreds of community colleges and universities in the last four decades and was recognized by the National Academic Advising Association in 1994 as one of two "classics in the literature on academic advising and one of the most cited in the literature."

Terry O'Banion's research and thoughtful analysis could not be timelier nor more urgent. Contributing to greater student success and, from there, higher completions, speaks to the core mission of community colleges and to the future of our nation. Over a long and distinguished career, he has been in the vanguard as a thought leader and a scholar. This work provides yet another vitally important resource for our colleges. And for our students, it may prove to be his most lasting legacy.

Walter G. Bumphus, CEO and President
American Association of Community Colleges

Preface

Terry U. O'Banion

I began my career in community colleges in 1960 as a very young dean of students at Central Florida Junior College in Ocala, Florida. Among all the student services we provided to our students, academic advising loomed as the most formidable challenge. After all, it was the one service we needed to provide to every student every term, and it was the prelude to classroom instruction. Our faculty colleagues could judge how well we did our job by how well students were prepared to begin their educational journey in the classroom.

All our student service staff were quite young and inexperienced, and we did not know very much about student services in general and even less about academic advising in particular. Early on we were strongly influenced by one of the few resources available, Mel Hardee's book, *The Faculty in College Counseling*, recognized nationally as the last word on the subject. Hardee believed that faculty members were the primary providers of academic advising, and, with no alternative voices to suggest otherwise, we subscribed to her beliefs. We did understand the importance of securing student feedback about their satisfaction with services, so we created an evaluation system and began to assess our experiments.

In our first year, we used all faculty as academic advisors. In the second year, based on student evaluations, we used only faculty who were interested in advising and who agreed to participate in training as advisors. In year three, we changed systems again and used only professional counselors to do the advising. In our evaluations, students expressed no more satisfaction with one model than another, so in the fourth year we allowed students to self-advise or see a counselor or faculty member of their choice. Once again, student satisfaction did not differ from any of the other surveys of the various models. Student satisfaction was quite low with every model we tried.

These outcomes puzzled me and led me to become a student of academic advising as my professional entrée into the world of student development. Later, I conducted the first national study of academic advising in the community college and made my first professional speeches on this topic. If the person who did advising made little difference to students, then what was the question? I soon figured out that the more important questions were, what is academic advising? What skills, knowledge, and attitudes are required by those who do the advising?

With this new perspective I began constructing and testing what emerged as the five steps that make up the process of academic advising in my model: exploration of life goals, exploration of vocational goals, program choice, course choice, and scheduling courses. I went a step further and suggested the skills, knowledge, and attitudes that advisors need to become effective academic advisors regardless of whether they are faculty, counselors, advising specialists, or students. *An Academic Advising Model* first appeared in the *Junior College Journal* in 1972.

In my experience, the two questions I focused on in the model were basic and simple, and I was surprised how the answers in a model I developed struck a chord in the field. That model was recognized in 1994 as one of two classic models by the National Academic Advising Association. American College Testing labeled the model as the "O'Banion Model of Academic Advising," and today a web search for that title results in 11,600 links.

The overarching mission of the community college today is student success, sometimes expressed as the *completion agenda*. Student success and the completion agenda are one and the same, except that the completion agenda comes with more sharply focused goals to double the number of students by 2020 who complete one-year certificates or associate degrees, or who transfer to a university. Never in community college history has such a goal been embraced by so many stakeholders from the White House to the state house and to hundreds of community colleges. Never in the history of the community college has such a goal had so much financial support from philanthropic organizations; the Bill and Melinda Gates Foundation alone has allocated $500 million to this effort.

As community colleges experiment with and engage in "promising and high-impact practices" to improve and expand the student success pathway to completion, academic advising is emerging as one of the most important programs in the student's experience. As stated in the original model: "The purpose of academic advising is to help students select a program of study to meet their life and vocational goals. As such, academic advising is a central and important activity in the process of education. Academic advising occurs at least once each term for every student in the college; few student support functions occur as often or affect so many students." It is not too much to claim academic advising as "the key to student success."

This book includes an updated version of the original model published in 1972. It also includes special chapters by leaders at the Center for Community College Student Engagement and the Community College Research Center. Most importantly, it includes four chapters by leading specialists in academic advising whose programs are among the most outstanding and exemplary academic advising programs in the country. These authors and I are pleased to share these informative chapters and innovative models with you and hope they will be useful in designing and redesigning academic advising programs to better ensure the success of our students.

ONE

An Academic Advising Model for the Twenty-First Century

Terry U. O'Banion

The year 2020 is the forty-eighth anniversary of Terry O'Banion's seminal article on a model of academic advising that was published by the American Association of Community Colleges in the Junior College Journal *in 1972. The model has been adapted by hundreds of community colleges and universities in the last four decades and was recognized by the National Academic Advising Association in 1994 as one of two "classics in the literature on academic advising and one of the most cited in the literature." The following article is an updated version of the original.*

Academic advising is the second most important function in the community college. If it is not conducted with the utmost efficiency and effectiveness, the most important function in the college—instruction—will fail to achieve its purpose of ensuring that students succeed in navigating the curriculum to completion.

    The purpose of academic advising is to help students select a program of study to meet their life and vocational goals. As such, academic advising is a central and important activity in the process of education. Academic advising occurs at least once each term for every student in the college; few student support functions occur as often or affect so many students. But although there is general agreement concerning the importance of academic advising for the efficient functioning of the institution and the effective functioning of the student, there is little agreement regarding the nature of academic advising and who should perform the function. The model proposed here defines the process of academic advising and outlines the skills and knowledge required of academic advisors who work with students through this process. It is a flexible model that can be adapted to the needs, resources, and culture of any institution of higher education.

THE PROCESS OF ACADEMIC ADVISING

The process of academic advising includes the following dimensions or steps: (1) exploration of life goals, (2) exploration of vocational goals, (3) program choice, (4) course choice, and (5) course scheduling. This is, of course, an ideal sequence of steps that moves a student through complex and significant explorations regarding key issues and goals to decisions about which courses to take and when to take them. Too often, colleges fail to connect this sequence for students; too often colleges give short shrift to the first two steps because of the pressing need to address the last three steps. If a college wants to improve the opportunities for student success—in a student's first term and through completion—the student must experience all five steps of the academic advising process.

Exploration of Life Goals

A sound and substantive college education should be a life-changing experience for students. In our haste to enroll students and move them to completion, we often fail to acknowledge the value and influence of our own experiences in college that opened up new worlds. We sometimes forget that college is a place for exploring new ideas, making new connections, and giving up worn-out views. First-generation college students from lower socioeconomic backgrounds may have no place other than college for this exploration.

A college education should ensure that every student has an opportunity to examine the questions, "Who am I? Where am I going? What difference does it make?" Few students come to us with any experience in exploring these essential questions. Such experiences provide a foundation for clarifying values and creating a satisfying philosophy of life—

goals that were basic to the general education programs of the 1950s and 1960s

The entire college experience and the entire college curriculum should be laced with these questions to provide any depth for the answers, but the exploration should begin as soon as a student first connects with the college. And the exploration must be a major feature of the academic advising process because that is the only function in which every student participates. Furthermore, the process of academic advising is incomplete unless the student has an opportunity to explore life goals as a prelude to exploring vocational goals.

College leaders recognize the importance of students exploring their life goals, and many programs and practices have been designed to provide this experience. In former decades, colleges created classic general education programs that included a personal development course as the heart of the program. In the late 1960s and the 1970s at Santa Fe Community College in Gainesville, Florida, the three-hour course "The Individual in a Changing Society" was required of every entering student. Many colleges have offered courses based on the Human Potential Seminar or on encounter groups.

Today the first-year experience and the student success course are the contemporary attempts to help students explore their life goals. In many of these courses, academic advising—along with assessment, orientation, career counseling, and registration—is folded into the experience to better connect the overarching life-goal questions with the immediate questions of which courses to take this term.

Although a course focused on life goals and questions provides more depth and time for students, the first sessions of academic advising have already taken place. If students are to benefit by this model of academic advising, then opportunities to explore life goals must be part of the process before students begin their course work. Such explorations should be more affective than intellectual. The following are promising practices colleges might wish to consider:

1. As soon as new students connect to the college and begin the admissions process, a special letter from the president or a key vice president should be sent welcoming the student to a college that provides a life-changing experience. As part of that experience students are required or urged to read a provocative book or article that comes with a few questions to stimulate discussions that will

occur in the required orientation sessions. The book might be provided free by the college supported by donations from an area business.
2. A similar opportunity for students to read and discuss life-goal issues could be created using technology in which each student would be required to work through a series of carefully crafted questions leading to an exploration of careers and vocational goals. Students would be required to complete this sequence before they meet with an academic advisor and before they register. If some of these experiences are explored in a college chat room, opportunities for networking are created that will help students begin to make connections with other students before they even meet on campus.
3. At a minimum, students should have an opportunity in advising or orientation sessions to explore some aspects of the essential questions about how they want to live their lives and the role college can play in that process.

Exploration of Vocational Goals

Vocational goals are life goals extended into the world of work. What a person is and wants to be (life goals) determines in great part how that person will earn a living and contribute to the general welfare of others (vocational goals). The relationship between life goals and vocational goals is intricate and complex; educators are understandably challenged in their attempts to help students make decisions in these areas. But because it is a difficult and often time-consuming process is no reason to avoid it. Many programs of academic advising flounder because they begin at step three with "program choice." It is assumed that students have already made choices regarding life goals and vocational goals when they enter the college—a questionable assumption for college students in general and a harmful and incorrect assumption for community college students in particular.

Although this model of the process of academic advising separates the exploration of life goals from the exploration of vocational goals for the sake of illustration, in practice the two steps cannot and should not be separated. It is certainly possible to separate the exploration of life goals into a series of experiences that stand alone, but here we are focusing on a process of academic advising that depends on a connection between the two. Clarifying life goals—as much as they can be clarified at this stage in a student's life—is essential in clarifying vocational goals.

In addition to student success courses and first-year college experiences, many colleges provide career assessment and career counseling opportunities for students to explore vocational goals. Although they occur after students have completed their first academic advising sessions, service learning experiences can be framed as significant opportunities for students to explore vocational goals.

As most experienced community college educators know, many community college students are not prepared to make decisions about vocational goals when they enter college. Once these students are clearly identified, they should be required to enroll in a prescribed program for "undecided students." If the college has a classic core of general education courses, this becomes the prescribed program.

As an alternative, a learning community that includes a student success course, an introduction to psychology, and a developmental or college-level writing course—or some appropriate cluster of courses—becomes the prescribed program. If the undecided student is enrolling in only one course, that course should be a student success course or an experience in which the exploration of life and vocational goals forms much of the content.

Research at the Community College Research Center–Columbia University (Scott-Clayton, 2011) suggests that community colleges offer too many options for students—especially for underprepared, first-generation college students—which may contribute to the low rates of student success. The research confirms that community college students will be more likely to persist and succeed in programs characterized by higher levels of "instructional program coherence," programs that are tightly and consciously structured like the prescribed program clusters noted in the preceding paragraph.

Program Choice

Once the college has provided an opportunity for life and vocational goal exploration through summer advising groups, occupational seminars, orientation programs, self-development classes, programmed guides, technology aides, experiential sessions, and so on, the student is ready to make a program choice. Even in a college or university offering traditional programs to a selected clientele, the process of choosing a program is challenging; in a community college offering a comprehensive range of programs to a great diversity of students, the process of choosing a program staggers the imagination. That is why requiring a prescribed and limited program for undecided students makes so much sense.

For students who are sure or have some idea of the program they want to pursue, the decision in favor of a specific program should emerge as part of the exploration of vocational goals. If students are sure of their choice of program, the academic advising process should move them efficiently and smoothly to the next steps. These students might be channeled to specific programs or departments such as nursing or criminal justice in which faculty advisors help them confirm their choices and in which they are oriented to careers in these areas.

As noted, the college should prescribe a limited program for students who are undecided. For students who are a bit unsure but who have inclinations toward a program, the advising process must help them design a program that will help them test their interests and offer options for changing their minds without losing credit. This is tricky business for the student and the advisor; the most effective advisors are required for this stage in the process.

Course Choice

Once the program is selected, students choose courses for the immediate term and perhaps for subsequent terms. Most colleges provide program guides that list the required courses, often noting the courses required by different transfer institutions. It is important to note prerequisites in selecting courses and to make sure students possess the competencies required for the courses. Advisors must be particularly sensitive in helping students who are unprepared for college-level courses understand the need for developmental courses and selecting a sequence that will lead to success.

There are many challenges in selecting specific courses for a term that requires knowledge and training on the part of personnel who assist in this process. Students who register late will not have as many choices as those who register early. Low-income and poorly prepared students tend to register later than other students, and they will be frustrated and disappointed when required or recommended courses are closed or not available at the preferred times.

Colleges committed to the Completion Agenda and the Student Success Pathway will require students to create personal development plans or road maps that can frame their choices and track progress as they navigate through the college. The plans and maps will include the courses required and elected for the program the student has chosen and must be accurate. They will also reflect courses transferred from other institutions. So, the choice of courses for a term is not a simple process, and, because advisors often sign off on these plans, this is a significant step in the academic advising process.

Scheduling Courses

Selecting the times courses are to be taken is often thought to be a simple task. But many community college students are unfamiliar with such concepts as semester-hour credit, transfer, grade-point average, developmental studies, and so on. They are often left on their own to figure out a schedule of classes to attend three days a week rather than the five to which they were accustomed in high school. While the scheduling of courses may appear easy to professional educators who themselves have registered and scheduled courses many times in their collegiate experiences, it can be a challenging experience to the nontraditional college student who attends the community college.

In 2007–2008, 83 percent of community college students worked while attending college; 42.9 percent worked full-time jobs and 40.7 percent worked part-time jobs (Staklis & Chen, 2010). Determining the times to schedule their courses for this great majority of students is a particularly daunting task. Many students are limited by the times they can take courses because they have family responsibilities, must arrange schedules around child care, and depend on other sources for transportation.

These five steps, then, are the dimensions of the process of academic advising: (1) exploration of life goals, (2) exploration of vocational goals, (3) program choice, (4) course choice, and (5) scheduling courses. Any well-conceived program of academic advising will include activities related to each of these dimensions. It may be possible for each of these dimensions to be explored in a single day; most colleges, however, are likely to consider the process of academic advising as continuous, beginning before the student attends class and continuing throughout the student's stay at the college.

THE SKILLS, KNOWLEDGE, AND ATTITUDES OF EFFECTIVE ADVISORS

To better understand the nature of the process of academic advising, it is important to consider the skills, knowledge, and attitudes required by the personnel who will assist students in each of the steps. The following is a tentative listing of such requirements:

1. **Exploration of life goals:** (a) knowledge of student characteristics and development, (b) understanding of decision-making process, (c) knowledge of psychology and sociology, (d) skills in counseling techniques, (e) appreciation of individual differences, (f) belief in worth and dignity of all students, and (g) belief that all students have potential.
2. **Exploration of vocational goals** (in addition to 1): (a) knowledge of vocational fields, (b) skill in interpretation of tests, (c) understanding of changing nature of work in society, and (d) acceptance of all fields of work as worthy and dignified.
3. **Program choice:** (a) knowledge of programs available in the college, (b) knowledge of requirements of programs (special entrance requirements, fees, time commitments), (c) knowledge of university requirements for transfer programs, (d) knowledge of how others have performed in the program, and (e) knowledge of follow-up success of those who have completed the program.
4. **Course choice:** (a) knowledge of courses available; (b) knowledge of any special information regarding courses (prerequisites, offered only in certain times, transferability; Does the course meet graduation requirements? What is the appropriate sequence for the university?); (c) rules and regulations of the college regarding probation and suspension, limit on course load (academic and work limitations); (d) knowledge of honors courses or remedial courses; (e) knowledge of instructors and their teaching styles; (f) knowledge of student's ability through test scores, high school record, and other factors; and (g) knowledge of course content.
5. **Scheduling courses:** (a) knowledge of schedule, (b) knowledge of the systems of scheduling and changing the schedule, and (c) knowledge of work and commuting requirements.

In addition to these requirements, all personnel who contribute to the process of academic advising must understand how to apply the technology used to undergird these five steps.

ACADEMIC ADVISING: A TEAM APPROACH

Historically, systems of academic advising have been designed as "faculty advising" systems or "counselor-based" systems; in contrast, the model described here strongly supports academic advising as an institution-wide, team approach. Academic advising is too important in the student success pathway to assign it to only one group in the institution. Personnel should be assigned to the process in terms of their skills, knowledge, and attitudes required for each of the five steps. Students; counselors; instructors; and special personnel such as student assistants, community volunteers, and advising specialists contribute to the process according to their competencies.

The student is responsible for decision making throughout the process. Students must be engaged in academic advising as full partners from the beginning. The student's role depends on experience, ability, and clarity of goals, but all students should be required to review prepared materials about vocational goals and program choices or to participate in special summer or preenrollment sessions to prepare for making decisions about programs and courses. Academic advising should be mandatory for every student every term, and the student should be prepared to meet his or her obligations.

In the team approach, counselors should have responsibility for helping students explore life and vocational goals. Ideally, new students should participate in this exploration in small personal-interaction groups during the summer. A programmed guide designed to help students explore life and vocational goals could be developed if face-to-face groups are not possible.

There is still a need to offer continuing opportunities for life and vocational goal exploration for returning students. Special seminars on occupations, experiential approaches to job sampling, service learning, voluntary encounter groups, learning communities, and student success courses are only a few of the ways the college can provide significant opportunities for students to discover meaning in their lives.

In addition to this direct involvement with students, counselors should prepare special information for instructors and students to clarify and support their roles in the academic advising process. Counselors should also provide staff development experiences for instructors and student assistants to improve and expand their competencies in academic advising.

The primary role of the instructor in the team approach is to assist students with choice of program and courses. Assuming the student has explored vocational goals and has selected a program, the student can then be assigned to an instructor in a department or division that reflects the career focus the student wants to explore. Instructors can provide a valuable experiential background for the student who explores a program in which the instructor is a professional. Some departments will provide an orientation to career clusters for groups of students; others will assign selected instructors to individual students to continue the process of program and course selection. In some colleges where counselors are assigned to departments or divisions, the counselors orchestrate these sessions.

Few instructors have the time necessary for staff-development activities designed to help them become effective advisors. If they teach full loads, participate on committees, and sponsor clubs and organizations, there is little time left for staff development. Unless there is an opportunity for instructors to learn about test interpretation, programs and courses, rules and regulations, transfer requirements, and many other aspects of the academic advising process, they cannot be expected to perform effectively.

If instructors are to participate in the process of academic advising in a professional way, then some important conditions must exist:

1. Academic advising must be recognized by the college as an important activity in the life of the institution. This means that instructors are rewarded for their participation perhaps by recognition of their contributions at the time of evaluation for rank and pay or in reduced class loads.
2. There must be a sensible student load. Some national studies have suggested that there be no more than fifteen advisees without a reduced teaching assignment.

3. There must be a continuing staff development program for all advisors, and a special, more intensive program for new instructors before they are allowed to participate.
4. There must be special concern for the advisory skills of instructors, which means that only those who qualify should participate.
5. There must be an adequate number of professional counselors available to handle referrals and the large number of students who are undecided about life and vocational goals.
6. There must be sufficient clerical help available to ensure that instructors have information when they need it and do not perform unnecessary clerical tasks.
7. Instructors must guard against using the system to recruit students into courses and programs not of the students' choice.
8. Cooperation and coordination must exist between the instructional program and the student personnel program to ensure the best use of all advising personnel in the best service to students.
9. Finally, there must be a program of evaluation by students, instructors, counselors, and advising specialists so that sensible modification can be made in a system that is ever-changing.

Many colleges, realizing there will never be enough counselors and full-time instructors for the academic advising of the great numbers of students who flock to community colleges, have created academic advising specialists. In some cases, the specialists are full-time staff with bachelor's degrees qualified to assist students with all five steps of the advising process; selected adjunct faculty could also be trained for this role. Students with a successful history in the college, students who have graduated and are looking for summer work, and community volunteers can be trained to assist with the final step in the process—scheduling courses. And some of these students and volunteers can be trained for step four—course choice. Counselors and instructors should never be assigned this task because it would constitute an ineffective use of well-paid and overqualified institutional resources.

CONCLUSION

The model of academic advising proposed in this article has been adapted by numerous colleges over the last forty years. The model has two key features that sustain its viability: (1) It defines academic advising as a system of five key steps that every student should navigate. (2) It outlines the skills, knowledge, and attitudes required of advising personnel for each of the five steps. Based on these two features, the model proposes that academic advising should be designed as an institution-wide, team approach using the competencies of counselors, instructors, and advising specialists, with the student taking responsibility throughout the process.

Academic advising occurs every term for every student and should be mandatory; it is the prelude to the central activity of the college—instruction. Certainly, the college should organize its resources to ensure that this prelude is sufficiently effective so that the student will have the greatest possible opportunity to navigate the student success pathway to completion.

REFERENCES

Scott-Clayton, J. (2011, January) *The shapeless river: Does a lack of structure inhibit students' progress at community colleges?* (CCRC Brief No. 25). New York: Columbia University Teachers College, Community College Research Center.

Staklis, S., & Chen, X. (2010) Profile of undergraduate students: Trends from selected years, 1995–1996 to 2007–2008 (NCES 2010). Washington, DC: US Department of Education, National Center for Educational Statistics. Retrieved from http://nces.ed.gov/pubs2010220.pdf

TWO

The Power of Advising in Community Colleges

Evelyn Waiwaiole and Courtney Adkins

In 1972, the editor of this book wrote, "The purpose of academic advising is to help the student choose a program of study" (O'Banion, 1972/1994, p. 10). Almost five decades later, at a time when many colleges are working to transform their institutions through guided pathways, advisors are still asked to do the same thing: help students choose a program of study.

However, although the core function of advising is the same, the role of advisors continues to evolve and expand. As colleges around the country are redesigning the student experience, job descriptions for advisors are changing. Advisors are being asked to outline each student's sequence of courses, deliver postassessment information, facilitate student orientations, offer various types of guidance to students (individually or in group settings), work with each student to create a personalized plan and continually review the plan to ensure that progress is made, outline information on resources and services the college provides, celebrate success points, assist with transfer and career planning, analyze student retention data, and take appropriate steps to promote student success. Advisors are asked to do all of this and more, while simultaneously building a relationship with every student they advise. More than ever before, advisors are crucial to student success.

GUIDED PATHWAYS AND ADVISING

But why is the role of advising changing so dramatically and how does this change fit into the redesign of the student experience? The answer is that community colleges are long past the time of having an open-door admissions policy as the primary mission. The focus now is on trying to ensure that those who walk through the doors are successful, which is defined as students' transferring or completing with the skills needed to thrive in a job that pays a living wage. This measure of success is the ultimate goal of the guided pathways movement. Essentially, if community colleges expect student outcomes such as persistence, retention, and graduation rates to change, then the way students experience college—and advising—has to change.

The Center for Community College Student Engagement (the Center) has worked with community colleges across the country since its inception in 2001. As part of this work, the Center asks member colleges to review both institutional and student engagement data. These data make clear that student outcomes can improve. For instance, at one college the Center worked with, 29.2 percent of students earned zero credits in the first term. At another college, as few as 4.3 percent of full-time students earned twenty-five to thirty credits in the first academic year. And at another college, only 17.1 percent of part-time students persisted to the subsequent fall term.

To address these concerns and others, colleges need to hear from students about what is working with advising and what isn't. To understand more fully how students experience advising, the Center added an academic advising module to the 2016 administration of the Survey of Entering Student Engagement (SENSE), a survey that helps colleges understand the early student experience. The survey was administered to 42,056 students at 102 colleges. Of those colleges, ninety-four administered the academic advising and planning item set to 39,784 entering student respondents.

An academic advising module was also added to the 2017 administration of the Community College Survey of Student Engagement (CCSSE), which students complete in the spring term. The survey was administered to 179,672 students at 297 colleges. Of those colleges, 188 administered the academic advising and planning item set to 113,315 respondents, of which 93,815 were returning students no longer in their first term of college.

Additionally, the 2017 Community College Faculty Survey of Student Engagement (CCFSSE) was administered at eighty-six colleges to 9,577 faculty. CCFSSE asks faculty members how they spend their time both in and out of the classroom and includes items about the role of faculty in the advising process. The remaining Center data referenced in this chapter are also from the 2016 SENSE administration and the 2017 CCSSE and CCFSSE administrations.

As well as working with colleges to collect student engagement data through its surveys, the Center has conducted focus groups with students at community colleges around the country for many years. To augment the advising data collected through the Center's surveys, several focus groups on advising were held with students and advisors.

Even as the role of the advisor becomes more complex, advisors continue to face the same long-standing challenges: high student-to-advisor ratios; the need to advise the majority of students in a short time frame; and competing demands for students' time, including work and child care.

But there is good news. More students now than in the past are meeting with advisors to establish academic goals and create plans. For example, in the 2011 SENSE administration, 56 percent of entering students said an advisor helped them set academic goals and create a plan for achieving them. In the 2016 administration, that figure rose eleven percentage points to 67 percent.

Clearly, more students are seeing advisors, discussing goals, and creating a plan to achieve those goals. When students are asked about how important advising is, 68 percent of returning students say it's very important, 24 percent say it's somewhat important, and 7 percent say it's not important. Perhaps emphasizing the importance of advising to students is something colleges want to consider.

Seventy-eight percent of returning students indicate they have met with an advisor. What is curious, however, is that only 62 percent of entering students have met with an advisor. Less than 50 percent of first-time-in-college students return to the same institution the following fall; therefore, this discrepancy suggests that early advising might contribute to increased retention (National Student Clearinghouse, 2017). And, when students don't see an advisor, they feel the effects. As one student said in a focus group, "For this semester, I didn't go to an advisor. I chose to skip, and I think I'm sort of paying the price for it."

Many colleges now require students to meet with an advisor. Entering students are more likely to be required to meet with an advisor than returning students. Among the 62 percent of entering students who report meeting with an advisor, 73 percent report being required to meet with an advisor before registering for classes their first term. Among the 78 percent of returning students who report meeting with an advisor, 51 percent report being required to meet with an advisor before registering for classes for the term. One student described required advising in a focus group by saying, "They do have it as a requirement. You have to meet with an advisor before you can sign up for classes. So that is a requirement. You can't even, actually, click on the classes until you meet with somebody."

Although entering students are more likely to be required to meet with an advisor, it's interesting that returning students are more likely to rely on college advisors than others for academic planning purposes. When asked who their main source of academic advising has been, 68 percent of returning students say it has been advisors or instructors. For entering students, only 47 percent report that it is college staff or instructors. Interestingly, 41 percent of entering students say friends, family, or other students are their main source of academic advising. For returning students, friends, family, or other students are only 21 percent of the main source of academic advising. It appears that students who have used the college's staff or instructors as advisors recognize the value of those services over that of friends, family, or other students; this is important information that should be shared with students before their first term.

Another tactic some colleges are taking to increase advising is to integrate advisors into the classroom to provide supplemental or ongoing advice. This is not happening at large scale, however. Just under one-quarter of students say an advisor came to one of their classes to speak about academic goals and planning.

CAREER COUNSELING AND TRANSFER ADVISING SERVICES

As colleges redesign the student experience with guided pathways in mind, they are focused on where the end of the pathway will lead students—and the hope that it will lead them to successful transfer or a career. Yet CCSSE and SENSE data confirm that most students are not using career counseling services regularly at their colleges. One college shared that 51.3 percent of students rarely or never used career counseling; another college reported that 73.1 percent of students rarely or never used career counseling. Moreover, another college shared that 40.3 percent of students *never* discussed their career plans with an advisor or faculty member.

Center focus group conversations support the student engagement data that show that students are not taking advantage of career counseling services. One student explained, "I know there are a lot of resources, but I think some of them—even the good ones—get shoved under the rug. The career success center is just in the corner. I'm super involved on campus, and I still really don't know what it is. I'm just being honest." Another student shared, "I'm not too sure if anybody told me about a career plan because I haven't gotten really in touch with the career plans or anything like that."

CCSSE data also indicate that half (50 percent) of returning students who report transfer as a goal have never used their college's transfer advising services. And in student focus groups, it was clear that students had different experiences when they did use transfer services. One student stated, "[My advisor] squeezed as many transfer credits as she could out of what I had previously done. I came out feeling very prepared for the semester and really excited about the classes I was going to take."

Another student had quite a different experience:

> Another thing that I would improve, I think, is, because this is a two-year school, I would expect the advisors to be more knowledgeable about transfer programs and about other schools that people plan on transferring to. We have the recruiters come in, sitting in the hallway right there outside, but you don't—when I've been in academic advising and talked about transferring before, my advisor's never really had any knowledge—not about the transfer process, but about, "Oh, yeah, I should put you in this because you wanna go do this here or something." I know that's a lotta schools to be responsible for, but even if you had some people in academic advising that were geared toward that and had that, and then you could be funneled over there to speak with them directly.

Colleges know the challenges students face, and restructuring the advising processes at their colleges to better meet the needs of their students is a top priority. Asheville-Buncombe Technical College in North Carolina redesigned its advising processes with a focus on transfer students, which is an important component of the college's work on guided pathways. Dennis King, president of Asheville-Buncombe Technical College, said:

> Our guided pathways project ensures that transfer students have the right courses for university transfer into major fields they selected with professional guidance. Also, because our students are directed into entry English and mathematics courses early, what they learn in these courses can positively impact other coursework. In all, we are satisfied that guided pathways are leading to more completers and more successful transfers. (Dennis King, personal communication, January 17, 2019)

A description of the college's transfer advising program follows.

Asheville-Buncombe Technical College (NC): Advising for Transfer Students Mandates Entering a Pathway

> At Asheville-Buncombe Technical College, 45 percent of students pursue transfer-related associate degrees such as an Associate in Science, an Associate in Arts, an Associate in Fine Arts, and an Associate in Engineering. An increasing demand for college transfer courses and a statewide articulation agreement with North Carolina's four-year colleges and universities led the college to develop a new approach to transfer advising.
>
> Thus, since fall 2016, all new students enrolled in a transfer program are supported through the Transfer Advising Center, which is staffed by a coordinator and two full-time advisors. Students enrolled in terminal degree programs (who do not intend to transfer) will continue with the college's prior advising model: Advising is required for all students to enable registration, and students are advised exclusively by faculty members in their individual programs of study.
>
> New students with a goal of transfer are assigned an advisor from the Transfer Advising Center during a transfer orientation session. All new transfer degree-seeking students are placed into a College Transfer Success course, which is mandated at the state level. In this course, students complete career exploration and then declare one of thirty-one pathways of study within the transfer degree programs. Career exploration includes researching careers of interest, investigating the credentials necessary for each career, and determining which four-year colleges and universities offer the credentials they are seeking.

After a student declares a pathway of study, the Transfer Advising Center assigns him or her a discipline-specific, full-time faculty advisor from within the student's chosen pathway. At this point in the College Transfer Success course, the student sets up an initial meeting with that advisor. Students are required to participate in this initial meeting before registering for courses for the following semester. The student works with this advisor each semester throughout his or her college career unless the student has more complex needs. In those cases, the student engages with Transfer Advising Center staff for guidance. If the student has more complex needs, he or she will receive guidance directly from the Transfer Advising Center's staff.

The College Transfer Success course is taught in a variety of time frames throughout the semester, including in eight-week and sixteen-week versions. Consequently, students choose pathways of study and are assigned a pathway-specific advisor at different points throughout the term. The college's goal is for all new students to select a pathway during their first semester. The full effect of the pathways project may not be realized for a few more years, but early indications are that pathway students enroll in and complete gateway English and math courses at a higher rate than non-pathway students, and they also accumulate credits faster than non-pathway students (Dennis King, personal communication, January 17, 2019).

WHAT STUDENTS SAY ABOUT GUIDED PATHWAYS AND ADVISING

As part of the Center's work on guided pathways, the Center conducted focus groups at three community colleges in the spring of 2017. At each college, three student focus groups were conducted with a total of seventy-one students, and one focus group was conducted with twenty-three faculty and staff involved in the guided pathways work at the college. As part of the focus group protocol, advising questions were included to better understand the guided pathways component focused on helping students get on a path. In reviewing the student responses to these questions, common themes emerged regarding guided pathways and academic advising.

Students Desire to Have an Academic Plan

During the focus groups, students expressed a desire for an academic plan, something tangible they can hold in their hand or see when they log on to the website, something that helps them map out where they are headed. They want to know how they go from point A to point B, and they want to be able to track themselves along the way to make sure they are staying on path. They recognize that academic plans also create a realistic timeline and show them when they will finish, which helps them to manage their time and expectations. One student described it this way:

> It's pretty hard to waver from the plan. When you're looking at all the classes, all you see is your program classes, so you really have to try hard to enroll in something that isn't part of your program. You have to know what either the class number is or the very specific class name if it's not part of your program. When I go online to register for my classes, there's my program name, and because I have some certificate programs too, there's a couple of those as well, but basically, we'll just focus on my associate degree. There's a little drop-down that I click on for my associate degree, and then there's four other drop-downs underneath that: Semester one, Semester two, Semester three, and Semester four. I just pick what semester I'm in if I'm following the four-semester plan, and then, so let's just say I pick Semester three. I'm in Semester three, so I click on Semester three, and then all the classes I need to take for Semester three, you just have to click on the name, and then you click "Add it to my shopping cart." Then, when you have all of those classes in your shopping cart, you just click "Enroll," and then it's like, "Are you sure you wanna enroll?" and then you accept financial responsibility for taking those classes, and then you're done.

Students Want to Be Assigned to an Advisor by Meta-Major, Major, or Program

Students were clear they want their advisor to be knowledgeable in their field of study. They want accuracy in the information they are being given. They also want to know when they contact their advisor that their advisor remembers them and the conversations they have had and can advise them based on those previous conversations. One student provided examples of when things do and don't go well in this area:

> It might just be because I'm in a smaller degree field, and none of the navigators, I guess, know anything about it. They're not communicating with the teachers at all. They argued with every single one of us in the degree program, until they talked with the teachers that we needed to take this nonexistent course that wasn't taught at the school anymore and just kept giving us this line of, "Oh, well, it's not offered next

semester, so we'll have to find you another class to take, or—and that this class that it's been replaced with isn't listed on your degree. If you want to take it, you can, but we'd really prefer you not to. . . ."

That's why, in my degree, we really enjoyed it when they switched over to everyone being under one advisor within—before each pathway. Because then we had one advisor who could know what was going on. Instead of us trying to explain to each individual advisor and—'cause when you have one person telling an advisor one thing, it doesn't really have as much of an effect as an entire group of people telling the advisor that, "No, you're wrong. You don't know what you're talking about."

> In speaking with the advisors in the focus groups, they too, want to be assigned to students by major. They indicated that fostering relationship with students is a large part of the job and assigning advisors by major helps them avoid the "jack of all trades, master of none" feeling.

Students Want Ongoing, Intrusive Advising

> At the Center, intrusive advising is called *inescapable advising*. But what does this really mean? It means that advising doesn't stop after the first semester or after a student has even registered for classes in the second term. Students were clear that they wanted to meet regularly with advisors. As one student said,

>> Well, I meet with my advisor a lot; I would say about twice a semester since 2013. I even met with my advisor when I took a semester off because I needed the break and I needed time to study for a certification exam. The first time, she contacted me to say, "Hey, let's talk about your plan." Actually, that was probably the second time that I met with her cuz the first time, we set up a plan. The second time, she wanted to make sure that that was still where I wanted to go with it. Since then, I meet with her about twice a semester to make sure everything's still where it needs to be and that nothing new came up cuz sometimes majors do—especially in education. The Department of Education will be like, "We need this new thing taught to the students to graduate," so it always keeps me on track that way. She's very helpful. I think there was one semester where I only talked to her once, and then she reached out again and was like, "We didn't talk at the end of last semester. How is everything?"

> Still another student said,

> The amount of times I've talked to my counselor was about a goal, I wanna say seven times, just so I'm on the right direction, or for signing up for classes, and just making sure that I'm going the right way, and that I'm not drifting away or taking the wrong things or going the wrong path.

Students notice when advisors go above and beyond to help answer a question for them (walked them to the financial aid office, called the bookstore during an advising session, followed up with the chair of the department until an issue was resolved, etc.). They also want to be taught how to monitor and take control of their own academic journey, to know about the safety nets built in to prevent them from getting off the path. Should they inadvertently start to get off track, they want to know interventions are put in place to immediately stop this from happening.

Logistics of Advising: The Responsiveness of Advisors and the Ease with Making Appointments Is Criucial

Throughout the focus groups, it was clear that students want timely responses via email, text, or phone—and they want to be able to have access to advisors. Some topics they discussed were whether there were walk-in hours, and if so, what the wait times were like. They also discussed scheduling advising sessions and how long they would have to wait to have their appointments, whether the next day or in several weeks because the advisor's calendar was full.

One student described her experience like this:

> When I first started to register for classes, I knew I wanted to be a teacher. I decided to wait [until the] very last minute, and I went to our front office. I waited two and a half hours with everybody else waiting, and I got to see a counselor who it took maybe fifteen minutes, [who] signed me up for all of my first classes, but it was definitely a long wait.

WHAT ADVISORS SAY ABOUT GUIDED PATHWAYS AND ADVISING

As part of the redesign work, not only is it key to listen to students and faculty, but clearly it's important to listen to advisors and hear their perspective on what is working and what is not working. In the focus groups with advisors, common themes surfaced, and from those themes, much can be learned about how to improve the advising process.

Advisors Know Relationships Are Key

One advisor spoke about the value of students seeing the same advisors and the importance of building a relationship with the advisee:

> I believe that one of the reasons that many students may be dissatisfied with advising is seeing different people throughout their journey in college. Not having that one constant person. The student stays with that one advisor from entry to completion. You build that relationship. You build that bond. You get to know the student. I think one of the beautiful things is seeing your student grow, like when they first started. They were scared. You developed the relationship. Then you see them, now, almost about to finish, and then see them walk the stage. That is, I think for me personally, one of the biggest accomplishments as an advisor. I joke with my students, I'm like I'm gonna change your life today. Because they don't realize this is the plan. There's a goal. I'm gonna help you get through it. Together, the sky's the limit.

Another advisor discussed how historically advisors were transactional, but now advisors are asked to build relationships with students:

> A really impactful change that we've made, at least on the Student Services side of things, is the idea of being relational with students, rather than transactional with students. Our student success navigator model is the main driving factor behind that. They have a really robust outreach and intervention plan that they follow in terms of connecting with students. As we think about supports that students need, and the way that we get them access to those supports, it comes from having a relationship with the student. It comes from understanding that they are struggling with Math, or that they're nervous about taking Psychology or Biology. Knowing that about the student and having the relationship that allows us to know that about the student. Then being able to refer them to the resources that we have. Those resources on campus have always existed, it was just a matter of making sure that the student knew and understood that they could get a free tutor or that supplemental instruction

was available in Math and some of these other things that we are pushing forward. Being relational, rather than transactional, has allowed us to embed those supports in another way, primarily through the student success navigators.

Advisors Are Invested in Guided Pathways

Advisors in the focus groups also spoke of the benefits to the changes in advising, specifically streamlining the onboarding process through guided pathways:

> One of the major benefits that I've seen for transferring to the pathway system is really a streamlining of the process for a student coming in. When they're looking through our course catalog, and if you're looking at a student coming in from high school, and you're looking to try to figure out, what do I need to take? In our old system, you had probably fifty different courses that you could choose from, and you had to pick and choose to put those together. We've really streamlined that process. I think it's a lot less ominous or [less likely to cause a feeling of] foreboding. Much less of a mountain for them to climb, to see that, okay, so I don't have to pick from all of this. It's kind of narrowed down. I can venture a little bit off of that. It's a little more manageable.

Another advisor shared how the step-by-step process ensured students were successful:

> Once a student has been accepted and admission is complete, they receive a letter with the name of their assigned advisor, and that's their person throughout their time here. That's the person that will customize their guided pathway. They've got to meet with them in their first semester, or they're not allowed to register for their second semester because there's a hold that's put on their registration process or on their transcript that they can't go further because we really feel it's very, very important that they sit down face to face with their advisor and look—and customize the pathway, talk about their goals, and also to address why are they here.

Another advisor spoke of the utility of the college's academic plan tracker because both the advisor and student are viewing the same information:

> The computer program that we utilize to track a student's progress is the exact same platform that a student can log into themselves to view their own progress. They can see a "timeline view," is what we call it.

Semester by semester, based on discussions with my navigator, based on my pathway, these are the specific courses that I'll be taking every semester. Of course, it is adjustable. If a student prefers to be a part-time student, prefers to isolate a course one-by-one or prefers to take more than what a pathway may recommend, it's just specific to the student. The student is also able to alter that plan, so that we may then approve their adjustments. Or they're able to communicate with us as navigators through that platform, but they're able to track their own progress in more of a degree audit type of way, as well as that's the area where they are comfortable registering through as well.

THE ROLE OF FACULTY IN ADVISING

Although some colleges are shifting away from the role of faculty advisors and are hiring full-time advisors, it's important to recognize that because faculty interact with students more than anyone else on campus, faculty will always advise students—whether formally or informally. Therefore, as colleges redesign for guided pathways, it's crucial to understand the faculty voice. When faculty are asked how important academic advising and planning are, 90 percent indicate they are very important. When asked how many hours faculty spend in a typical seven-day week advising students, 58 percent of part-time faculty said one to four hours, and 62 percent of full-time faculty said one to four hours.

HOW COLLEGES ARE REVAMPING ADVISING SERVICES

Although advisors discussed many topics in the focus groups, the two key themes focused on the importance of relationships and guided pathways. Another consistent take away in this work is that there is no silver bullet. Colleges are approaching this redesign work in many different ways.

- Jackson College in Michigan requires students to complete an intake form asking about their lives, similar to what a person may do when visiting a doctor's office.
- Alamo Colleges in Texas created Alamo Advise, a defined plan for advisors to reach out to students prior to their arrival at one of its five campuses. Advisors continue to connect with students at specific milestones—students are required to meet with an advisor

when having earned fifteen, thirty, and forty-five credit hours. If students do not meet with an advisor, then a hold is placed on the student's account until the advisor gives the student a pin number. The pin is needed for a student to register for classes.
- St. Petersburg College in Florida completely redesigned the student advising experience, moving from a transactional experience to a relational experience. Advisors completed 120 hours in career training to help prepare them for this change.
- Skyline College in California developed SparkPoint, a financial education and coaching center to improve college connection and completion by mitigating economic disparities.

Paris Junior College in Texas hired additional advisors who now operate under a caseload model. The registration system has been programmed to ensure students register for classes in their program maps. The college president, Pam Anglin said, "As we began the implementation of Guided Pathways, we quickly realized much of our success in pathways would come from early and intrusive advising. The use of Student Success Coaches responsible for advising and tracking an assigned group of students was chosen to assure a level of personal attention that would help improve student retention and success" (P. Anglin, personal communication, March 6, 2019).

All five of these colleges approached the redesign of advising in a unique way, and all five have seen positive results from the changes they have made.

Redesigning for guided pathways is not easy work, and it is not stand-alone work. Taking a deeper look at colleges and the work they are doing shows that there is not a "one size fits all" model. Very different approaches to the redesign work from Community College of Philadelphia (Pennsylvania) and Cleveland State Community College (Tennessee) illustrate how different methods can create positive outcomes.

Community College of Philadelphia (Pennsylvania): More Intensive Advising Correlates with Increased Persistence

> As part of its guided pathways reform efforts, the Community College of Philadelphia implemented a new advising model for the 2016–2017 academic year. The college shifted from a structure in which faculty advised all students on a part-time basis to a model in which students are advised by full-time advisors. At the same time the college adopted

a more intensive advising model, which has an intake process that clarifies student goals and career direction and includes progress tracking and individually designed support. The new onboarding process involves engaging students from application to enrollment, with educational planning starting when students register for their first semester. The interaction of students and advisors early in their onboarding to the college enhances connections to further increase students' persistence rates.

The college presently employs eleven full-time advisors who are assigned to individual students and also assists with walk-in advising requests. The full-time advisors were initially assigned to students in the largest curricula at the college: health care, liberal arts, business, computer information systems technology, psychology, and justice programs. In fall 2017, 65 percent of first-time students ($N = 3,699$) at the college were assigned to a full-time advisor. Now the Academic Advising Department advises all new students.

The full-time advisors provide extensive and proactive academic advising to students using a number of formats: one-on-one, group, and virtual advising through Skype. They also stay in touch with students via e-mail; phone; and Starfish, the college's retention software. All contacts with students are documented in Starfish, and advisors use this program to refer students to tutoring and other academic support services as needed. Using Starfish, advisors also can track whether students have followed through with referrals.

Every student who sees an advisor creates an educational plan, and students then register based on this plan. In addition to meeting in the advising offices, advisors attend sections of the college's first-year experience course (which is required for all students in health care, business, and liberal arts) to begin the students' creation of their educational plans.

The new advising model, along with other reforms, such as the implementation of first-year experience courses, appears to be increasing persistence.

- Among students who were assigned an advisor, the fall 2017 to spring 2018 persistence rate was 75.4 percent ($N = 2,406$), compared to 69.1 percent ($N = 1,293$) for students who did not see an advisor.
- Among first-time college students who were assigned an advisor, the fall 2017 to fall 2018 persistence rate was 49.4 percent ($N = 2,406$), with students not assigned to an advisor persisting at 42.5 percent ($N = 1,293$) (G. Generals, personal communication, January 17, 2019).

Cleveland State Community College (Tennessee): Graduation Rates Rise after Advising Overhaul

Cleveland State Community College launched a new advising model in spring 2013 and moved to full-scale implementation in fall 2013. The new model revamps almost all aspects of the advising process.

- **Who gets advised?** The college requires all credential-seeking students regardless of enrollment status to participate in advising each term, and students are not allowed to register for courses until they see an advisor, who gives each student a PIN number to access registration.
- **Who advises?** New students are required to attend an orientation event in which initial career exploration takes place and after which initial academic advising occurs. After the orientation, students choose a major or academic pathway and then are assigned a faculty advisor in that pathway. Although most students experience one-on-one advising with their assigned faculty advisor, they can also use drop-in services in the Advising Center, which is staffed by full-time faculty members and a few select staff, all of whom have completed the college's intensive online training.
- **Content of advising.** To ensure a consistent level of quality, the college developed checklists for each category of students with whom advisors meet. Students must also enroll in a first-year seminar (preferably in the first semester), which covers exploration of career choice in more depth, academic advising and planning, and other related topics.
- **Intensity of advising.** Advising sessions for new students may take more than an hour as faculty tailor each advising session to the individual needs of the student, whereas sessions for students with academic plans in place may take as little as fifteen minutes.

Cleveland State developed this new advising approach after the governor announced the state's Drive to 55 initiative, which aims to increase degree completion to 55 percent of all Tennesseans by 2025. It was launched as part of the college's 2011 accreditation work. The college used both Center survey results about advising and career counseling and internal data such as the Survey of Advising to assist in the implementation of new advising models. The college also hired a consultant from the National Academic Advising Association (a professional organization for higher education advisors) to review advising policies and procedures.

After implementing the new approach to advising, the three-year graduation rate for first-time, full-time students increased from 14 percent ($N = 718$) for fall 2010 students to 22 percent ($N = 774$) for fall 2013 students. The most recent cohort entering in fall of 2015 completed at a rate of 26 percent ($N = 775$) by 2018.

There was also an increase in the number of first-time, full-time students earning twenty-four credits in the first year, from 10 percent ($N = 784$) in 2012 to 30 percent ($N = 743$) in 2016. Similarly, 32 percent of students ($N = 489$) in 2017–2018 completed at least twenty-four credits.

In addition, students are reporting a more positive advising experience. In 2014, 59 percent ($N = 56$) of students surveyed said the advising experience was easy and helpful. In 2017, that figure rose to 78 percent ($N = 206$) and in 2018 was 76 percent ($N = 67$).

CCSSE 2018 survey results at Cleveland State indicate that 85 percent of students had met with an advisor by the middle of the spring term, and of these respondents, 58 percent had met with an advisor twice or more. Furthermore, nearly half of students reported meeting with the same advisor each time. The college uses results such as these to target areas for improvement and hopes to continue to see an increase in relationship building between advisors and advisees.

"We love to study our data," says Denise King, vice president for Academic Affairs, "but it is the personal relationship we build intentionally with each student that means the most and we believe, contributes so highly to their satisfaction and success" (Denise King, personal communication, January 17, 2019).

A major shift is in the planning stages for intensifying this relational support for students through the use of professional advisor or success coaches assigned by Career Community (an academic focus area) to serve students through the first twenty-four credit hours with faculty mentors or advisors guiding students from twenty-four credits through graduation and job placement or successful transfer. Through this effort, Cleveland State Community College aims to push past the national averages for completion, even as that number continues to rise (W. Seymour, personal communication, January 17, 2019).

ADVISORS ARE AN INTEGRAL PART OF THE PATHWAY TO SUCCESS

As the advising role changes to encompass much more than registering students for class and as the advising process continues to move from one that is primarily transactional to one that is relational, community college student outcomes will change. In fact, these outcomes are already changing. The front door at community colleges is still open, but the good news is that at many colleges, there is now a defined pathway for more students to succeed and accomplish their goals by transferring or entering the workforce. Advisors are a large part of this pathway to success for students.

REFERENCES

National Student Clearinghouse Research Center. (Spring 2017). *Snapshot report: First-year persistence and retention.* Retrieved from https://nscresearchcenter.org/wp-content/uploads/SnapshotReport28a.pdf

O'Banion, T. (1994). An academic advising model. *NACADA Journal,* 14(2), 10–16.

To review the Center's survey instruments and academic advising modules, see the following:

Community College Survey of Student Engagement (*CCSSE*): www.ccsse.org/aboutsurvey

Community College Faculty Survey of Student Engagement (*CCFSSE*): www.ccsse.org/CCFSSE

Survey of Entering Student Engagement (*SENSE*): www.ccsse.org/sense/aboutsurvey

Academic Advising and Planning Module:

CCSSE: www.ccsse.org/join/options.cfm#standard

SENSE: www.ccsse.org/sense/aboutsurvey

THREE
A Framework for Advising Reform

Serena Klempin, Hoori Santikian Kalmakarian,
Lauren Pellegrino, and Elisabeth A. Barnett

College advising and related student supports are intended to help students navigate their way to credential completion and beyond, yet resources for deploying these services, especially at community colleges, have typically been constrained. In addition, traditional advising systems do not seem to adequately address the needs of many of today's students, a fact brought into relief when considering that graduation rates continue to be low; only 39 percent of students who entered two-year public colleges in the fall of 2012 completed a degree or certificate within six years (Shapiro et al., 2018).

Although advising reform is often embedded in institution-wide efforts to improve student success,[1] perhaps the most comprehensive approach for reforming advising services at broad-access colleges has been developed through the *Integrated Planning and Advising for Student Success* (iPASS) initiative, supported by the Bill and Melinda Gates Foundation. In 2012 and again in 2015, the foundation awarded grants to forty-five colleges to support the launch and use of advising technologies and to strengthen advising practice. Beginning in 2015, the initiative also engaged technical assistance partners, including Achieving the Dream[2] and Educause.[3]

iPASS was developed to transform how colleges and universities approach student advising. The goal of iPASS is to provide students with a more seamless, holistic advising experience that leads to improved student outcomes. Under iPASS, institutions select new technologies and learn how to use them, collect new data, help faculty and advisors integrate the data and technologies into their practice, and ultimately change the way they interact with students. To accomplish this, each college participating in the first round of the initiative received a grant totaling approximately $100,000 over two years, and each college participating in the second round received a grant of up to $225,000 over three years. Additionally, each college participating in the second round of the initiative received assistance in change management, in rethinking their advising and other student support strategies, and in selecting and deploying appropriate technologies.

The Community College Research Center (CCRC) has been examining the implementation and outcomes of a number of recent advising redesign efforts, including iPASS (Fletcher, Grant, Ramos, & Karp, 2016; Jaggars & Karp, 2016; Kalamkarian & Karp, 2015; Karp, Kalamkarian, Klempin, & Fletcher, 2016). As a research partner in the iPASS initiative, CCRC conducted qualitative implementation studies at six iPASS institutions from the 2012 cohort of grantees (Karp, Kalamkarian, Klempin, & Fletcher, 2016).

Following a second round of funding in 2015, CCRC undertook qualitative implementation studies at an additional twelve iPASS grantee institutions as well as descriptive analyses of key performance (student outcome) indicators at all twenty-six of the 2015 cohort colleges. In partnership with MDRC, CCRC is also currently engaged in an experimental evaluation of an enhanced approach to iPASS at three of these institutions.

Based on some of this research as well as a review of the literature, CCRC developed an evidence-based framework for advising redesign (Karp, Kalamkarian, Klempin, & Fletcher, 2016). This chapter presents the key tenets of this framework and shows how it may be of use to colleges considering a redesign of their advising practice.

The chapter begins by defining the key principles of an ideal advising experience for students based on theoretical and empirical literature. The remainder of the chapter describes how these principles, incorporated in the framework, may be implemented. The information and recommendations shared here are derived primarily from qualitative research conducted during the years when iPASS reforms were being developed. The focus is on lessons learned and examples of practice in the participating colleges.

ENVISIONING AN IDEAL ADVISING EXPERIENCE

Advising reforms are efforts to implement high-quality, effective practices that support students as they work toward completion of a credential. As part of the iPASS approach described previously, the SSIPP framework was developed to articulate a set of principles that have the potential to create an ideal advising experience (Kalamkarian, Boynton, & Lopez, 2018). SSIPP refers to a *sustained, strategic, integrated, proactive,* and *personalized* approach to advising.

This conceptualization assumes that advising should not be a one-time or a purely transactional experience; rather, advisor engagement throughout the complete student experience at the institution is encouraged, along with interactions with other student support staff. Although the iPASS model emphasizes the use of technology to increase the efficiency and effectiveness of advising practices, the SSIPP framework can be implemented, at least to some extent, without extensive use of new technologies.

The SSIPP framework is largely derived from a review of the literature on institutional services and interventions, including academic advising, that aim to help students navigate college and take into account academic and nonacademic aspects of the student experience. The literature examined comprised 128 reports, articles, and books, including both empirical studies and seminal theoretical contributions (Karp, 2011; Karp & Stacey, 2013).

Table 3.1. Principles of the SSIPP Advising Framework

- **Sustained** support is offered to students throughout their tenure at the college.
- **Strategic** deployment of advising resources is achieved by creating systems that differentiate support for students depending on their needs and interests.
- **Integration** of advising with other student supports as well as other aspects of the college experience is likely to serve students more effectively.
- **Proactive** advising is needed to make sure that all students are reached; students who most need support may not come and ask for it.
- **Personalized** advising is achieved when advising is offered by someone who knows a student well and is attuned to the student's needs and interests.

FACILITATING ORGANIZATIONAL CHANGE

In practice, advising systems at open- and broad-access colleges[4] face resource limitations that make it challenging to achieve the principles outlined in the SSIPP framework. At these institutions, caseloads for advisors can exceed seven hundred advisees. Advisors may not have sufficient time in a semester to meet with all of the students in their caseload (Jaggars & Fletcher, 2014; Karp, 2013). Moreover, advising systems often function independently from other student service departments and offices, including career counseling. These conditions make it challenging to offer students the coherent support experience proposed under the SSIPP framework (Karp, 2013).

However, by using strategies developed by colleges associated with the iPASS initiative, some colleges have been able to move closer to the ideal. Importantly, this requires much more than adopting new technologies. Adriana Kezar's seminal work on organizational change offers a theoretical foundation for understanding the nature of the change necessary to achieve a substantially improved advising experience. Kezar (2013) defines *structures, processes,* and *attitudes* as three areas of focus that are required to enact substantive change. *Structures* include organizational policies, systems, and staff hierarchies. *Processes* are defined as the ways that an organization enacts plans and policies. *Attitudes* are the assumptions or perspectives of key individuals that are upheld by the organization.

CCRC research findings lend support to the importance of Kezar's three dimensions of change in the context of advising redesign. To achieve a system of advising that is consistent with most or all of the tenets of the SSIPP framework, institutions need to attend to (1) structures that facilitate implementation of each of the five SSIPP principles at scale, (2) processes for enacting the high-quality support envisioned by the framework, and (3) attitudes that view advising as primarily focused on guiding students toward the fulfillment of their education and career goals (Karp, Kalamkarian, Klempin, & Fletcher, 2016).

IMPLEMENTING THE FIVE PRINCIPLES OF THE SSIPP FRAMEWORK

Institutions may choose to enact the SSIPP framework in numerous ways. In the following sections, practices undertaken by colleges exemplifying each of the five principles of SSIPP are highlighted as a way for readers to gain insights into how the framework can be implemented. In doing so, references are made to Kezar's three dimensions of change. Pitfalls are also considered that can occur while undertaking this important but challenging work.

Sustained Support: Regular Touch Points

Colleges typically offer a range of advising supports for incoming students, such as new-student orientations, individual career planning and advising sessions, and freshman seminars (Karp, 2013). Yet evaluations of these one-time supports generally find that, although they may be useful in the short-term, they do not lead to improved long-term student success (Karp & Stacey, 2013; O'Gara, Karp, & Hughes, 2009). Orienting students to college and providing them with information and guidance about potential academic pathways at the start of their student experience is simply not enough to ensure that students will stay on track to completion. Alternatively, a design for sustained advising aims to engage students in supportive activities throughout their tenure at the college.

One example of sustained support involves establishing a range of communication platforms (e-mail, phone, in-person, or virtual meeting) and hiring an increased number of institutional staff (advisors, counselors, peer mentors, and other supplementary staff) to regularly communicate with enrolled students. Regular touch points such as these, if meaningful to the student, can help guide students at various junctures in their college pathway and, when needed, create the opportunity for more intensive intervention.

Structural Dimension

Sustained engagement with students requires institutions to establish a clear plan and timeline for touch points that can include both cohort-wide and more targeted and even personalized messages. For example, as part of their advising redesign, North Central Community College[5] outlined a set of informational communications for different kinds of students. Informational messages to the full student population are sent out biweekly and provide details on institutional resources, including child care and transportation options. A subset of students identified as more likely to struggle are sent additional messages providing guidance and encouragement. The college also offers extra communications early in the semester for students with self-reported challenges or those who appear to be experiencing distress based on academic performance or other data.

This kind of regular engagement with students requires both personnel resources and structural changes. Given their resource constraints, institutions are thinking creatively about how to bolster the capacity of the advising staff. Technology tools can enable advisors to carry out a wider range of communications in a limited amount of time. At both Western State and Southern University, advisors use communication technologies that allow them to create email messaging campaigns that include an embedded link that recipients can use to schedule advising appointments. These tools also make it easier for advisors to target communications to subsets of their advisees and to quickly follow up with those who do not act to schedule an appointment.

Well-crafted and efficient communication with students is facilitated by the creation of templates for phone or email messages. Advisors and other support staff at colleges involved with iPASS report that, although they want to be able to customize messages, some standardized language serves as a useful and potentially time-saving starting point. Moreover, templates can encourage a type of engagement that an advisor or support provider had not previously used or considered. And messaging can be customized. For example, at Southern University, advisors felt strongly that communications that carried their names needed to sound like them; consequently, as the institution implemented its communication plan for continuing students, advisors maintained the ability to customize these messages as they saw fit.

Process Dimension

Even with structures that facilitate regular engagement with students, implementation of an outreach plan depends on advisors' and other support staff's time and capacity. Changes to advising practice may require advisors and other support staff to make changes in their norms and processes. For example, at institutions with technology tools that make it easier to reach out to students, advisors and support staff need to shift from using manual or traditional email platforms in day-to-day activities to the newer technology platform, a process that can require training and perseverance.

Attitudinal Dimension

Enactment of an advising model that involves sustained student engagement may require a shift in institutional culture and perceptions. Advisors, other support providers, and administrators interviewed at iPASS colleges expressed a range of views on the purpose of advising and student supports. A number of them felt that advising and student supports were intended almost exclusively to intervene if and when students exhibit academic or nonacademic risk. At these institutions, implementing a sustained advising experience for students required getting advisors, support providers, and administrators to reflect on ways that students' circumstances may change over time, making it necessary to maintain some engagement with students to monitor and respond to their needs.

Potential Pitfalls

There is a fine line between sustained communication and inundating students with endless messages and requirements for too much facetime. Colleges should use caution in reaching out to students to avoid getting tuned out entirely. Additionally, not all students need the same level of support. It is recommended that colleges have a plan for communications and advising sessions, but it may also be prudent to give advisors flexibility in how they implement the plan and encourage them to use their best judgment on how to support students, particularly as they get to know them over time.

STRATEGIC SUPPORT: ADVISING REDESIGN IN A GUIDED PATHWAYS CONTEXT

Guided pathways is a good example of how colleges are taking a strategic approach to improving student support and advising as a key part of institution-wide reforms. About 250 community colleges across the country have undertaken the work of guided pathways as part of a national reform movement that is framed as enabling colleges to "fundamentally redesign their programs and support services in ways that create clearer, more educationally coherent pathways to credentials" (Jenkins, Lahr, Fink, & Ganga, 2018, p. 1). This multifaceted reform approach is growing in popularity as community colleges seek to help students reach their educational goals in a timely manner with little to no excess credits.

Although the work of guided pathways is complex and iterative, taking at least several years to fully implement, the principles are simple: (1) Provide students with coherently conceived programs of study, (2) help students choose a program and develop an individualized academic plan, (3) keep students on the path, and (4) ensure that students are learning (Bailey, Jaggars, & Jenkins, 2015).

Academic advising is a crucial component of guided pathways implementation, with many colleges facilitating collaboration between academic and student services departments to refine programs and develop strong student supports. Key activities include creating maps that chart out well-conceived course sequences through programs of study, investing in technology and additional student support personnel to improve capacity, and restructuring systems and procedures to support students from the time they consider applying to college to the time they graduate or transfer (Jenkins, Lahr, & Fink, 2017).

Structural Dimension

One of the early steps that colleges take in implementing guided pathways is developing meta-majors, which are broad categories of disciplines that serve as organizing "buckets" for programs at the college.[6] Although many colleges and states require students to declare a major or program of study on their application, some colleges allow students to enter a meta-major before formally deciding on a program or major. In either case, colleges can leverage meta-majors as a way to help students develop an academic and professional identity through onboarding, program exploration opportunities, and campus events.

Many guided pathways colleges organize onboarding activities and first-year experience courses by meta-major, enabling students to learn about a limited number of related programs (versus the consideration of hundreds of programs) and offering students an early opportunity to develop a support network of peers, faculty, and advisors, all of whom are affiliated with a specific meta-major. Within this structure, advisors and faculty are collaborators in supporting students, ideally establishing systems that allow them to communicate regularly about student goals and progress within each student's broad area of interest.

Advisors and faculty may meet regularly to ensure consistency in their interactions with students or stay in touch through the use of technology platforms. The use of meta-majors can increase the opportunities for students to receive coherent guidance and support from knowledgeable, trusted individuals and, in turn, develop confidence and agency in navigating their educational journey.

Process Dimension

In addition to onboarding and early support, advisors in a guided pathways context closely monitor students' progress and intervene when students need help. To facilitate this, many guided pathways colleges (as well as others) use technology to alert advisors when students are veering off their educational pathway, such as when they attempt to take courses outside of their plan.

When an advisor is alerted that a student is deviating from the pathway, the advisor can reach out to that student and offer help. Some advisors use an advising syllabus that outlines advising learning outcomes or provides a set of guiding questions to foster critical thinking during advising sessions. This may help students overcome hurdles to progress along their chosen pathway or even change their education and career direction.

Attitudinal Dimension

Strategic advising in a guided pathways context may require changes in norms and perspectives among advisors, faculty, and other college personnel about who is responsible for student support at what moments. The roles of faculty and professional advisors[7] differ by college, but a common understanding of how to best guide students along a pathway is needed. Structured collaboration between advisors and faculty enables both groups to build knowledge of each other's roles, develop a common language for student support, and establish norms around working as a team.

Potential Pitfalls

Although considered a crucial step in guided pathways development, advising redesign in this context is challenging. Some colleges may assume that only faculty or only advisors should be involved in advising redesign, a situation that can create confusion and, in some instances, foster resentment among groups at the college. Another common misstep is trying to rush a reform by applying a "quick-fix" technology or hiring new employees without clarifying the strategic intention of those decisions. However, decisions that must later be amended can be costly, cause delays, and negatively affect buy-in across stakeholder groups.

Undertaking Guided Pathways Advising Reform at Midwest Community College[8]

Before embarking on advising redesign as part of its guided pathways work, Midwest Community College (MCC) had four professional advisors for more than 7,000 students. Students were not assigned to advisors, and appointments were available on a walk-in basis only. The wait times for students were long, and because there was no case assignment, students were often asked to repeat themselves and were sometimes receiving inconsistent information. Because of those challenges, many students registered and planned for courses on their own, only to find themselves in trouble later with excess, nontransferrable credits and needless student loan debt.

Since beginning its guided pathways work, the college has hired ten professional academic advisors and four financial aid advisors to support students. With the advisor-to-student ratio down considerably, MCC implemented structures and processes that enable advisors to be strategic in their roles and provide students (and even prospective students) with substantial support and information when needed.

Although MCC advisors were originally trained as generalists, they are now assigned to one of the six divisions (corresponding to MCC's meta-majors) at the college and operate as specialists. Additionally, MCC advisors have been trained as certified career counselors so they can provide early and ongoing career exploration and preparation opportunities.

Because advising is structured by division, division faculty and advisors have developed strong working relationships, attending each other's meetings and contacting one another with student-related questions or concerns. To monitor students' progress, advisors meet with every student prior to registration every semester and are expected to interact with students several times over the course of a semester. If students want to change their educational plans, they are required to meet with an advisor to facilitate a smooth transition and ensure that excess credits are avoided or kept to a minimum.

In terms of onboarding, the college has implemented strategies to retain students from application to enrollment and provide them with tools and resources that help them to be successful early on. After a prospective student applies to the college, an advisor reaches out to welcome him or her to MCC and confirm or help the student explore a direction. The college has also changed from using a group orientation to an individual orientation, with students meeting with their academic advisor and financial aid advisor separately, one-on-one and face-to-face. Although this structure keeps all advisors very busy in the early days of the semester, MCC faculty, staff, and administrators contend that students are far better equipped to "hit the ground running" than they have been in the past.

The first-year experience course at the college, while facilitated by a faculty member or advisor, is a collaborative effort between faculty and advisors. As part of the course, faculty and advisors from each division host an event where all faculty and advisors within that division set up exhibits, give presentations, and talk with students about the programs and career opportunities that are available. Students build their full educational plan (to graduation) with their advisor during the course.

The early and ongoing opportunities for faculty and advisors to work together to support students have been helpful to MCC. Prior to its guided pathways work, faculty and advisors operated more or less autonomously. Both groups recognized early on that increased collaboration would support their own work as well as offer more seamless and personalized support for students. They also saw improvements in earned credits during the first year and felt that students were responding positively to intensive and customized advising services.

INTEGRATED SUPPORT: COLLABORATING ACROSS THE COLLEGE

The SSIPP framework calls for advising that is integrated within and across both the academic and student support domains of the college. In many colleges, both faculty and professional advisors share advising responsibilities but may work in "silos," which limits communication and the potential for collaborative relationships. In these cases, close coordination of the work can make sure that the right support options are available to students at each point in their journey through college. In addition, coordination among student support providers of various types (e.g., advising, financial aid, career counseling) can result in better-aligned services.

Structural Dimension

Effectively achieving integration of support services depends to a considerable degree on the leadership structure of an institution. Colleges that undertake advising reform typically have leaders that clearly and frequently articulate their vision and are adept at bringing together autonomous units within the institution to support student success in a cooperative and meaningful way. In addition, revisions to policies (for example, guidelines for working with students, the monitoring of student progress, and record-keeping procedures) are often required to recalibrate operations and better coordinate services.

As one might expect, colleges may rely heavily on technology for integrating student supports, as software systems are designed to enable stakeholders across the college to communicate with one another and with students effectively and efficiently. Adopting new technology is among the most difficult challenges for colleges undertaking advising redesign, but it can be vitally important when there is a need to bring together information from disparate sources and share it with multiple stakeholders.

Process Dimension

With the implementation of structural change to provide integrated student supports comes the need to put processes in place to operate within the new structure. Colleges need to consider the ways in which faculty, staff, and college leaders will interact with one another (meetings, emails, case notes) and topics for discussion (reviews of data, discussions of individual student progress) and how this affects responsibilities and work flow. Stakeholders also need training on how to use new technology and how to optimize its functionality to achieve good collaboration.

Attitudinal Dimension

In colleges that have made considerable progress in the integration of advising and other student services, college leaders communicate effectively with stakeholders about the need for reform and provide a compelling vision for the future. At the same time, there are typically many opportunities for faculty and advisors to take ownership of specific changes that are required. With broad participation in structuring the reform, revised practices are more likely to fit well with other ongoing processes, and buy-in among stakeholders may be higher.

Potential Pitfalls

Integrating advising, especially when employing new technology, takes considerable time; the work can lose momentum if leaders and key personnel scale back communications or fail to address resistance. When different groups at a college are accustomed to functioning independently of one another, it can be particularly difficult to set up and maintain systems for regular communication, with or without technology.

It is worth emphasizing that incorporating new technology to accommodate integration is often extremely challenging, and a number of colleges have experienced disappointments. Advising-related technologies are expensive, and colleges may not have the resources to purchase all of the functionalities of a system that could potentially make integration easier. Further, the information technology departments at community colleges are sometimes small, leaving colleges to rely on vendors for support. If a college cannot afford to pay for that support or does not receive the support it expects, successful adoption of the tool may never happen.

Integrating Student Supports at Great Lakes Community College

Great Lakes Community College (GLCC) is a small community college serving 2,500 students. Prior to participating in the iPASS initiative, GLCC's student support systems were uneven, with students accessing advising on an as-needed basis and receiving faculty advising services as a "hand-off" from professional advisors well into the students' tenure at the college. In an effort to reach students more intentionally, the college implemented a case management system in which professional advisors interact with students who exhibit risk factors. It also restructured the faculty advising model so that students and faculty engage with one another from the time of first enrollment. These changes required that faculty and advisors work closely together to ensure that students are connected with the right supports at the right time to address their needs at each stage of their education.

In terms of technology, GLCC purchased tools from a vendor to assist with education planning, identifying students at risk through predictive analytics, and sending early alerts. Ideally, these tools would work seamlessly with the college's existing technology and enable professional advisors and faculty advisors to provide consistent support. Unfortunately, after more than two years of effort to solve problems, GLCC decided to cancel its contract with the vendor and reexamine its technology strategy. This was a costly and frustrating experience for the college and serves as a cautionary tale about working with external entities to introduce or combine complex technology systems.

Despite this, the efforts to integrate student supports by professional and faculty advisors were viewed as a success. In the process of working to incorporate technology tools, both groups came to understand more about each other's cultures and roles, and they developed clearer ideas on how to complement each other. They came to think of themselves as a "unified front" in supporting students early and often. The widespread buy-in was in large part attributable to the college administrative team who successfully transmitted the goals and vision of the project, and to the midlevel leaders who supported faculty and staff on the front lines with ongoing and consistent communication and helpful professional development opportunities. Today, the college is working with its older technology products and talking with new vendors about potential options.

PROACTIVE SUPPORT: EARLY ALERTS

Access to advising and other student supports often depends either on students taking the initiative to seek out services or is reserved for students who have failed to meet certain benchmarks. A proactive approach to advising, on the other hand, seeks to shift the impetus for engagement from students to advisors and faculty members. Rather than waiting for students to seek help, an effort is made to reach out to students at key moments in their college tenure and particularly when they appear to be struggling.

Technology-based early alert systems can enable proactive advising. They are designed to provide an efficient means of flagging and supporting students who show signs that they may be struggling and to provide encouragement to students who are doing well by recognizing their successes. Alerts can be triggered in two ways.

Some early alert systems can automatically mine institutional data pertaining to students' performance. More commonly, individual faculty members and other staff manually raise an alert by flagging a student in the early alert system. In either case, once an alert has been triggered, the system generates an automatic message to the student and the student's advisor or other student support staff. The advisor and others then follow up with the student to offer assistance while also documenting their actions as well as the student's response.

Structural Dimension

Before launching an early alert tool, colleges need to make a series of decisions about what data should be used to trigger alerts, what categories or types of alerts should be available (e.g., poor attendance, low grades, high grades, missing an assignment, behavioral concerns), how to frame the content and tone of the messages that are sent to students and advisors or other support staff after an alert has been triggered, and the degree to which these messages should be personalized. (Experience shows that even factors such as the wording of the subject line or how the sender of the email is identified may influence whether students read it.)

Furthermore, colleges need to decide who will raise manual alerts (only faculty members, or also advisors and other student services staff) and when alerts will be raised (at predetermined points each semester or any time as needed). Colleges also need to establish technical protocols related to raising alerts, such as whether the system should consolidate multiple alerts raised by multiple individuals for the same student into a single message. Finally, colleges should clearly specify to faculty and staff whether raising alerts is an expectation or is voluntary.

Equally important are well-defined guidelines outlining the appropriate type and level of response for different alerts. For example, a single alert related to a late assignment probably represents a relatively low level of concern that could be addressed through a standardized email reminding the student about the assignment and the effect on their grade of not completing it, while multiple alerts indicating a student might be in danger of failing one or more classes might warrant a more high-touch and personal response, such as a text message or phone call.

Other needed guidelines for responding to alerts include identifying which individuals are responsible for following up with which students and establishing criteria for closing alerts by deciding what constitutes successful follow-up. Additionally, the technology tool used to generate alerts should permit advisors to document the actions taken in response to alerts and to determine which college personnel will have access to that information.

Further, to understand whether early alerts are being used as intended, it is helpful to develop a system for tracking information such as the number of alerts raised and successfully closed and student use of support services after receiving an alert. This information can then be compared with course-level outcomes and student persistence data to examine the relationship between early alerts and student success.

Harbor University's experience with implementing early alerts offers a good example of the importance of taking the time to invest in the development of clear guidelines. The college realized early on that setting up an early alert tool would require reevaluation of the existing inconsistent system for assigning students to advisors to ensure that every student had a designated advisor to whom alerts could be sent. Additionally, the college had to rapidly develop a protocol for triaging alert responses after the number of alerts raised during the first semester the tool was launched—17,000 alerts for 4,000 students—far exceeded the initial expectation of 2,000 alerts (Klempin & Karp, 2018).

Process Dimension

Guidelines and protocols create a system for using early alerts, but for the approach to be effective, faculty members, advisors, and student services staff must commit to using them as intended. This can be aided by communicating clear expectations and norms. For example, at Bluffview Community College, faculty are asked to raise alerts within the first few weeks of the semester, informed by short assignments that do not have a large effect on students' grades but still provide useful information about students' progress.

At the same time that faculty members are engaging in new processes such as scheduling when and how they assess student work, advisors and other student services staff should be monitoring alerts and responding to them, engaging in targeted outreach, and sharing case notes that faculty members can then review to see what came of the alerts they raised. Together, these actions can establish systems that foster the development of a coordinated network of support for students.

Attitudinal Dimension

To fully commit to engaging in the use of early alert systems, college faculty and staff must believe that their actions can have a positive influence on student success. Further, they must embrace responsibility for proactively identifying and supporting students who may be struggling. Without attention to underlying attitudes and concerns, it is easy for misperceptions about the purpose of early alerts to flourish. For example, at Oceanview Community College, faculty members were concerned that raising too many alerts would reflect poorly on their ability as instructors. At Bluffview Community College, faculty members were initially reluctant to adopt early alerts because it felt like tattling on students. To address this, Bluffview gave two faculty members release time to serve as early alert coordinators who facilitated dialogue between faculty and the early alert implementation team.

Potential Pitfalls

An early alert tool can provide a powerful means for promoting proactive support, but neglecting to consider structural, process, and attitudinal dimensions runs the risk of overemphasizing technology as the solution without attending to the human side of the intervention. To avoid this problem, Oceanview Community College developed a training program to help faculty members recognize what kinds of issues are best addressed personally with students and which should be elevated to an advisor or other student services staff member via an alert.

Finally, early alert messages are meaningless if students never read or respond to them, and they could even do harm if students are discouraged by them. Thus, it is crucial to understand students' perspective on early alerts. To avoid the risk of unintended consequences and to ensure that students perceive the messages as authentic and supportive, research should be conducted on students' opinions about using an early alert system and on their interpretations of messages.

PERSONALIZED SUPPORT: CASE MANAGEMENT

Personalized support is fundamentally about tailoring student services to students' unique interests, motivations, and needs to ensure that they receive the resources that will help them succeed. Not all students will require the same type or level of support at the same time. Thus, personalized support requires developing an understanding of students as individuals.

One strategy for personalizing support is to use a case-management model that leverages technology to enable a more individualized approach to student support. In a personalized case-management model, advisors are assigned to work with the same students over time and given access to a comprehensive record not only of students' academic standing but also of any results of nonacademic assessments (e.g., results from surveys about career interests or from questionnaires about interests in student services) or case notes that exist.

As opposed to a system of drop-in advising where all advisors serve as generalists and primarily focus on immediate requests for assistance from students, a personalized case-management model calls for getting to know students and following the same students' progress over time. Using this approach, advisors have the opportunity to address not just short-term needs such as course registration for the following semester, but also longer-term goals. Sessions may involve, for example, helping students understand the connections between their coursework and career interests, working with students to develop time-management strategies, or discussing challenges with finding child care.

Structural Dimension

Creating the structures to establish a personalized case-management model first involves implementing guidelines for assigning students to advisors. Students may be assigned to advisors based on any number of factors. They may be assigned randomly (e.g., alphabetically by last name), by the broad program area or meta-major (e.g., liberal arts, health sciences) in which the student is enrolled, by the student's major (e.g., history), or by the student's involvement in particular activities or their background (e.g., athletes, veterans).

Encouraging advisors to specialize in a small number of programs of study or a single meta-major may allow them to develop expertise in areas that are most relevant to their students, making it more likely that students will intentionally seek out meetings with their assigned advisor. Additionally, assigning students to advisors should include consideration of caseload size. Inevitably, larger caseloads will make it harder for advisors to deliver personalized support.

There should also be consideration of expectations for the frequency of contact with students. Colleges should carefully weigh the pros and cons of various advising policies such as placing holds that do not permit students to register before receiving advising or requiring an advising appointment as an assignment for a first-year experience course. Students may benefit from more contact with advisors; they also may be harmed if they are unable to register for courses in a timely way while waiting for an advising appointment. It is also important to embed regular advising touch points when case managers will reach out to students. For example, advisors may conduct targeted outreach to those students who have reached crucial progression milestones, such as earning a certain number of credits toward completion (Karp & Stacey, 2013).

To ensure that advisors have the capacity and skills they need to capitalize on a case-management model, colleges may want to build advisor schedules that allow them to set aside blocks of time for scheduled appointments with students. As noted previously, colleges may also want to use a technology tool that gives advisors easy access to pertinent student information such as education plans, course grades, alerts raised by faculty members, and shared case notes.

Process Dimension

Using a case management approach can often mean that advisors need additional preparation for advising sessions to make sure they are familiar with each advisee's interests and issues. They must be familiar with the technology required to review students' academic standing and to maintain good advising records. Ideally, advisors should prepare for sessions by reviewing multiple data sources as well as their own case notes to identify where students may be struggling and what types of guidance or resources might be most appropriate. After the session, advisors typically use technology to document the main issues discussed, make referrals to other student services, and follow up on whether students use the services.

Attitudinal Dimension

Implementing a personalized case-management model requires advisors to consider aspects of mentoring and counseling as a core part of their role, in addition to the provision of academic guidance. Colleges implementing the model should thus foster an institutional culture that prioritizes individualized student support as a key mechanism for promoting student success.

Potential Pitfalls

Establishing a case-management model through which all students receive personalized support is by no means an easy task. Budget constraints, large advising caseloads, and other challenges related to assigning students to advisors can all pose structural barriers to personalized case management. In particular, ensuring that advisors have the time they need to provide personalized support often presents a significant challenge. What is more, students may not understand the personalized case management approach or find it uncomfortable or intrusive. Thus, it is important to communicate the purpose of this model to students and encourage them to engage in this more comprehensive and sustained advising process.

Implementing Personalized Case Management at Southwestern Community College[9]

The case management advising model at Southwestern Community College (SCC) was intentionally designed to complement the college's adoption of guided pathways reforms. Advisors are assigned to work with students within a meta-major or a specific program of study. SCC established seventeen discrete "touch-point" periods during which advisors reach out to students. Examples of these include directly following placement testing to discuss students' scores and options for course pathways, when students are making financial aid appeals, and when students wish to drop a course. Advising is also required and enforced with a registration hold after students have completed fifteen, thirty, and forty-five credit hours.

To monitor students' academic progress, the college adopted an education planning tool that advisors can use with students to create individual success plans, including all the courses needed to complete a credential in the chosen program of study. In addition, the college provides numerous professional development opportunities for advisors to ensure that they have the technical knowledge and skills they need as well as a grounding in counseling techniques.

The director of advising at the college describes their advising model as one that encourages advisors to be intentional in reaching out to and keeping track of students and believes that "with relationships comes greater success." Advisors appreciate the fact that their role on campus is highly valued and that they have been allowed to become experts in specific program areas. In addition, surveys have shown that students' satisfaction with advising has significantly increased since the college adopted the model.

FINAL THOUGHTS

The SSIPP framework provides a foundation for reflecting on existing advising and student support systems in a college to consider reforms that improve student experiences and outcomes. The path to implementing change may vary from college to college, and there may be variation in the specific reforms made. However, it can be helpful to know what other institutions have accomplished and challenges they have faced. In this chapter, there are summary descriptions of ways that each of the SSIPP elements have been implemented in colleges studied by CCRC staff; these may inform others wishing to improve local practice. In addition, colleges may want to consider structure, processes, and attitudes when planning for change. Attending to these dimensions can improve the likelihood of high-quality implementation.

REFERENCES

Bailey, T. R., Jaggars, S. S., & Jenkins, D. (2015). *Redesigning America's community colleges.* Cambridge, MA: Harvard University Press.

Bettinger, E. P., & Baker, R. B. (2014). The effects of student coaching: An evaluation of a randomized experiment in student advising. *Educational Evaluation and Policy Analysis, 36*(1), 3–19.

Fletcher, J., Grant, M., Ramos, M., & Karp, M. M. (2016). *Integrated Planning and Advising for Student Success (iPASS): State of the literature* (CCRC Working Paper No. 90). New York, NY: Columbia University, Teachers College, Community College Research Center.

Jaggars, S. S., & Fletcher, J. (2014). *Redesigning the student intake and information provision processes at a large comprehensive community college* (CCRC Working Paper No. 72). New York: Columbia University, Teachers College, Community College Research Center.

Jaggars, S. S., & Karp, M. M. (2016). Transforming the community college student experience through comprehensive, technology-mediated advising. *New Directions for Community Colleges, 2016*(176), 53–62.

Jenkins, D., Lahr, H., & Fink, J. (2017). *Implementing guided pathways: Early insights from the AACC pathways colleges.* New York: Columbia University, Teachers College, Community College Research Center.

Jenkins, D., Lahr, H., Fink, J., & Ganga, E. (2018). *What we are learning about guided pathways, part 1: A reform moves from theory to practice.* New York: Columbia University, Teachers College, Community College Research Center.

Kalamkarian, H. S., Boynton, M., & Lopez, A. G. (2018). *Redesigning advising with the help of technology: Early experiences of three institutions.* New York: Columbia University, Teachers College, Community College Research Center.

Kalamkarian, H. S., & Karp, M. M. (2015, August). *Student attitudes toward technology-mediated advising systems* (CCRC Working Paper No. 82). New York, NY: Columbia University, Teachers College, Community College Research Center.

Karp, M. M. (2011). *Toward a new understanding of non-academic student support: Four mechanisms encouraging positive student outcomes in the community college* (CCRC Working Paper No. 28). New York: Columbia University, Teachers College, Community College Research Center, Columbia University.

Karp, M. M. (2013). *Entering a program: Helping students make academic and career decisions* (CCRC Working Paper No. 59). New York: Columbia University, Teachers College, Community College Research Center.

Karp, M. M., Kalamkarian, H. S., Klempin, S., & Fletcher, J. (2016, July). *How colleges use Integrated Planning and Advising for Student Success (iPASS) to transform student support* (CCRC Working Paper No. 89). New York, NY: Columbia University, Teachers College, Community College Research Center.

Karp, M. M., & Stacey, G. W. (2013). *What we know about nonacademic student supports.* New York: Columbia University, Teachers College, Community College Research Center.

Kezar, A. (2013). *How colleges change: Understanding, leading, and enacting change.* New York: Routledge.

Klempin, S., & Karp, M. M. (2018). Leadership for transformative change: Lessons from technology-mediated reform in broad-access colleges. *The Journal of Higher Education, 89*(1), 81–105.

O'Gara, L., Karp, M. M., & Hughes, K. L. (2009). Student success courses in the community college: An exploratory study of student perspectives. *Community College Review, 36*(3), 195–218.

Scrivener, S., & Weiss, M. J. (2013). *More graduates: Two-year results from an evaluation of Accelerated Study in Associate Programs (ASAP) for developmental education students*. (Policy Brief). New York: MDRC.

Shapiro, D., Dundar, A., Huie, F., Wakhungu, P. K., Bhimdiwala, A., & Wilson, S. E. (2018, December). *Completing college: A national view of student completion rates—Fall 2012 Cohort (Signature Report No. 16)*. Herndon, VA: National Student Clearinghouse Research Center.

NOTES

1. Many colleges undertake these efforts using the "guided pathways" institutional reform approach, which focuses on establishing clear program pathways for students and helping them develop and follow plans that take them through programs of study to graduation and careers.

2. Achieving the Dream is a nongovernmental organization that provides coaching and other resources to more than 220 colleges in 41 states (www.achievingthedream.org).

3. EDUCAUSE is a nonprofit organization that supports implementation of information technologies at member institutions (www.educause.edu).

4. *Broad-access colleges* are defined as two- or four-year institutions that accept a majority of applicants.

5. Pseudonyms are used for the names of the colleges throughout this chapter.

6. For example, the meta-major of Business and Public Services Technology may include programs in accounting, culinary arts, and criminal justice.

7. "Professional advisors," unlike "faculty advisors," are typically full-time, dedicated advisors who are not considered full-time faculty. Faculty advisors are full-time faculty members who also serve in a formal advising role. Many colleges use a "split" advising model where professional advisors work with students for a period of time before they are transitioned to a faculty advisor. There may also be variation across disciplines; programs may use only professional advisors, only faculty advisors, or a split model.

8. Midwest Community College was not an iPASS college.

9. Southwestern Community College was not an iPASS college.

FOUR
LifeMap 2.0

The Evolution of a Developmental Advising Model at Valencia College

Ed Holmes, Evelyn Lora-Santos, John Britt, and Kathleen Plinske

Valencia College (Valencia), a community college serving the greater Orlando area, has multiple campus locations in both Orange and Osceola counties in central Florida. Serving more than 70,000 students each year, Valencia offers a two-year associate in arts degree intended to prepare students for baccalaureate transfer, more than thirty different two-year associate in science degrees to prepare students for employment in specialized careers, and five baccalaureate programs to allow students to continue their education beyond the associate level in specific, career-focused fields. Approximately 75 percent of degree-seeking students at Valencia intend to earn an associate in arts degree, and the majority of students intending to earn a baccalaureate degree plan to transfer to the University of Central Florida (UCF).

Although UCF has become increasingly selective in its freshman class admissions, Valencia has developed a unique partnership with UCF called *DirectConnect to UCF*. Through DirectConnect to UCF, students who complete an associate in arts degree from Valencia are guaranteed admission to UCF. This partnership has grown to be so popular with students that nearly one-quarter of graduates from UCF are transfers from Valencia (UCF Office of Institutional Research, 2016).

Over the last decade, Valencia has faced a unique set of challenges. Between 2006 and 2016, Valencia's enrollment grew by nearly 50 percent, during which time funding support from the state did not keep pace. In addition, recent legislative changes prohibited community colleges in Florida from requiring developmental education and required a significant overhaul of the general education curriculum. Furthermore, changes to both lower-division and upper-division course requirements have created more complex degree pathways.

Fortunately, Valencia has had a strong developmental advising model in place since the early 2000s, which helped the college effectively respond to these challenges. This chapter provides an overview of Valencia's developmental advising model, of the process by which adjustments were made to the model to respond to emerging challenges, the ways in which the model supports students from their transition into Valencia through their graduation, and of the institutional systems that support the model.

HISTORY OF LIFEMAP

The advising model at Valencia College is shaped by the developmental advising philosophy known as LifeMap, which first emerged in the mid-1990s. During this time, Valencia was exploring what it meant to be a "learning-centered college" (Klingman, 2008). The college reviewed its systems with a focus on two learning-centered questions: "How does this action improve and expand student learning? How do we know this action improves and expands student learning?" (O'Banion, 1997).

As a result of this review, the LifeMap model for developmental advising emerged, which was informed by Frost's (1991) ideas that students' motivation in class was influenced by their faculty members' understanding of their goals, that advising is a form of teaching, and that "advising alliances" can be important to support student success (Romano, 2013).

LifeMap is designed to promote students' social and academic integration, education and career planning, and the acquisition of study and life skills. LifeMap recognizes that most students begin college with only a vague notion of their career goals and a limited understanding of higher education systems. With a goal of developing students' self-sufficiency, LifeMap is modeled after a five-stage student life cycle (Shugart & Romano, 2006). These five stages are:

- College Transition
- Introduction to College
- Progression to Degree
- Graduation Transition
- Lifelong Learning

It is through these stages that advisors help students learn how to become responsible for their educational journey. LifeMap intends for students to be active participants in the student-advisor relationship, and as students progress through each stage, they begin to take more responsibility while the advisor begins to play a less active role in the relationship.

Contextual Changes

In the twenty years since the initial development of LifeMap, Valencia has grown to serve a significantly larger and more diverse student population. In addition, state legislative changes required developmental education reform and altered general education requirements. Moreover, the creation of several different options to allow students to meet their lower-division and upper-division course requirements created additional flexibility but made some advising decisions less straightforward. These challenges prompted Valencia to revisit its LifeMap model in 2014 and work toward the development of a design for LifeMap 2.0.

Institutional Growth

Valencia has grown in size, distribution, and organizational complexity during the last twenty years. In 2000, Valencia served just over 40,000 credit students at four campus locations. By 2018, the number of credit students had grown to over 60,000 enrolled at six campus locations. One of Valencia's "Big Ideas" is that students who make a personal connection with a faculty or staff member early in their academic trajectory are more likely to be successful (Shugart, Phelps, Puyana, Romano, & Walter, n.d.). An enrollment increase of 50 percent stretched the college's capacity to maintain its commitment to personalized service and relationships, and a key design element of LifeMap 2.0 was a desire to foster meaningful personal connection between students, faculty, and staff.

Moreover, the addition of campus locations challenged Valencia's organizational structure. Valencia employs a matrix-management model in which the deans of students at each campus report directly to the college-wide vice president of student affairs but have a "dotted line" reporting relationship with the campus president. In the original LifeMap model, advisors reported directly to the deans of students, but growth in Valencia's scale and distribution necessitated a different organizational model that introduced directors and assistant directors of advising at each of Valencia's largest campuses.

Legislative Changes

One of the motivating factors behind the creation of LifeMap was Valencia's dissatisfaction with the levels of success experienced by students who required developmental education courses (Romano, 2013). Prior to 2013, community colleges in Florida were allowed to mandate assessment testing, which would measure students' abilities in math and English. The results of these tests determined whether students were ready for college-level courses; if students did not demonstrate the skills necessary to be successful in college-level coursework, students were required to enroll in developmental courses. Students at Valencia who required developmental coursework demonstrated increasing levels of success after the implementation of LifeMap.

However, Florida Senate Bill 1720, passed into law in 2013 amending Section 1008.30 of the Florida statutes, allowed for any student who entered a Florida public high school in 2003 or later and who graduated from a Florida public high school the option to enroll in college-level coursework at a state college or university without demonstrating readiness for college-level coursework via a standardized assessment. Many faculty and staff were concerned about students for whom developmental coursework would have been beneficial before entering into college-level coursework and believed that advising would play a crucial role in helping students select courses in which they would have the greatest likelihood of success.

In addition to this significant reform related to developmental education, the state of Florida also made substantial changes to general education requirements. Prior to 2014, state colleges and universities had the authority to identify the specific courses that met general education requirements. However, Florida House Bill 7135, passed into law in 2014 amending Section 1007.25 of the Florida statutes, created a general education core requirement that consisted of a limited set of course options within each general education discipline that would be consistent across every state college and university.

As a result of this change, Valencia's general education curriculum included both core and institutional course requirements, creating a more complicated degree pathway for students. The design of LifeMap 2.0 had to take into consideration how advising could help address these challenges created by recent legislative changes.

Development of More Nuanced Student Pathways

In addition to significant changes related to developmental education, Florida Senate Bill 1720, passed into law in 2013 amending Section 1008.30 of the Florida statutes, also mandated the development of "meta-majors" to serve as academic pathways for students. The corresponding rule approved by the State Board of Education identified the following eight meta-majors:

- Arts, humanities, communication, and design
- Business
- Education
- Health sciences
- Industry/manufacturing and construction
- Public safety
- Science, technology, engineering, and mathematics
- Social and behavioral sciences and human services

In addition to identifying the meta-majors, the corresponding state rule also specified the gateway mathematics courses that would be required for each meta-major. In response, Valencia developed "math pathways" to help students select the appropriate mathematics courses for their intended field of study (Math Pathways, n.d.).

Florida's meta-majors have specific course requirements, as do baccalaureate majors. To help students select courses that meet not only Valencia's degree requirements but also the baccalaureate requirements students will face once they transfer to a university, Valencia developed both pre-majors and transfer plans.

Meta-majors, math pathways, pre-majors, and transfer plans are useful tools to help students with the course selection process and to progress toward completion of a degree as efficiently as possible. Although these tools work well for students who are steadfast in their academic program selection, they can create complications for students who change their mind about their program of study after their first semester in college. The design of LifeMap 2.0 addressed how to help students find their purpose early in their academic trajectories while also supporting them if they change direction.

DEVELOPMENT OF LIFEMAP 2.0

Recognizing that these contextual changes challenged the original LifeMap model, Valencia committed to revisiting LifeMap. Nearly twenty years in the making, it was time to consider a redesign, revisiting the central, learning-centered questions: "How does this action improve and expand student learning? How do we know this action improves and expands student learning?" (O'Banion, 1997).

Valencia has developed an institutional habit of using the architectural design model as an approach to collaboration for major systems design work. The value of the architectural model to design is that it focuses first on arriving at an understanding of and agreement on principles and purposes before arriving at a solution. Just as the first step of an architect's process is to understand the owner's requirements and develop an "architectural program" for a new building, Valencia's design process begins with the development and articulation of design principles that outline what the college is trying to achieve and how it will know whether the design solution is successful (Shugart, 2014).

LifeMap 2.0 Design Principles

As Valencia embarked on a redesign of LifeMap, the college created the following design principles for LifeMap 2.0:

1. A long-term personal connection between students, advisors, and faculty provides the foundation for effective advising.
2. There is purposeful alignment between academic advising and new student experience (NSE) initiatives to help increase student persistence, progression, and degree completion.

3. Student success is achieved by infusing intentional developmental advising checkpoints throughout the stages of LifeMap. Advisors, faculty, and students are proactive participants in the process.
4. Identifying learning outcomes and creating an assessment plan is imperative to the design. Assessment results are to be used to make improvements to advising curriculum.
5. Advising is a learning experience with shared responsibilities between students, advisors, and faculty. Communication between advisors, faculty, staff, and students is essential to the success of our students.
6. Advising provides new students with meaningful cocurricular activities, which allow students to discover, create, and reinforce their academic pathways.
7. Students are required to participate in activities that result in the selection of their major, program, and career.
8. Systemic inclusion of LifeMap College Success Skills is essential.
9. A coordinated effort to develop and sustain external and internal partnerships is essential to the long-term success of students.
10. Staff must intentionally employ advising theory and best practices from across the country whenever possible.

These design principles are the blueprint for the LifeMap 2.0 model at Valencia, which focuses on a deeper personal connection between advisors and students. As the model continues to develop and grow, and as the college faces new challenges, the design principles will guide decisions about the work. Valencia's directors of advising review these principles annually to ensure they are still relevant to the model and the needs of the students.

Catalysts for the Design Process

As Valencia was preparing to revisit its original LifeMap model, several opportunities served as catalysts for the design process. As part of its decennial review for the Southern Association of Colleges and Schools Commission on Colleges (SACSCOC), Valencia was required to develop a quality enhancement plan (QEP). Valencia leveraged this opportunity to accelerate the design of LifeMap 2.0. In addition, Valencia received a Title III and a Title V grant from the US Department of Education, which further accelerated the design and implementation of LifeMap 2.0.

Quality Enhancement Plan

At Valencia, like many colleges, the highest student attrition occurs within the first fifteen credit hours of a student's experience with college; most student failures (and institutional failures) are at the "front door" (Shugart, 2016). Research suggests that inadequate knowledge about how to navigate college, lack of financial and family support, and failure of students to identify a clear academic path may be to blame for this high percentage of attrition (Cho & Karp, 2013; Scott-Clayton, 2011).

As Valencia developed its QEP, as required by SACSCOC for reaffirmation of accreditation, the college decided to focus on its proverbial "front door." Valencia faculty and staff carefully and deeply examined students' early experiences at the college, wrestling with the challenge of providing a highly personalized experience for students at a large, distributed institution.

Valencia's QEP outlines the development of an NSE for all degree-seeking students at Valencia. The outcomes of the NSE are that all students:

- Complete an NSE course.
- Achieve their first fifteen college-level credits.
- Acquire academic behaviors associated with success in college.
- Make the connection between college and finding purpose in life.
- Establish Valencia as a place for learning and community.

The NSE includes a required, three-credit, college-level course that provides an extended orientation to college, integrated student success skills, and career and academic advising. To deliver the NSE course to all students, Valencia developed a hybrid twelve-month, full-time NSE faculty position. NSE faculty serve as instructors teaching the NSE course during the fall and spring while they serve their cohort of students as an NSE advisor during the summer. NSE faculty are also integrated within student affairs during the summer months and between the fall and spring terms, when they serve as advisors and as new-student orientation facilitators.

Figure 4.1 outlines Valencia's updated student success pathway, beginning with all degree-seeking students meeting with an advisor during the face-to-face sessions of new-student orientation and being advised to register for the NSE course (or its alternative) as well as other gateway courses. Soon after the development of the QEP was underway, Valencia received a Title III grant that helped conceptualize students' continued success pathway in engaging with their assigned advisors (Transition to Degree Programs and Graduation, Career Placement, and Transfer).

Title III Grant Funding

When Valencia received a Title III grant in 2012, the college was able to expand the NSE. Title III funds permitted the college to move the work forward quickly and to focus personnel time and resources on the design and pilot of new strategies including:

- Small group intake advising during new-student orientation
- Installation of educational planning software
- Implementation of appointment scheduling software
- Certification of faculty members in LifeMap developmental advising strategies
- Improvement of advisors' capabilities by establishing a consistent and comprehensive advisor training program
- A thirty-credit-hour required advisor check-in milestone

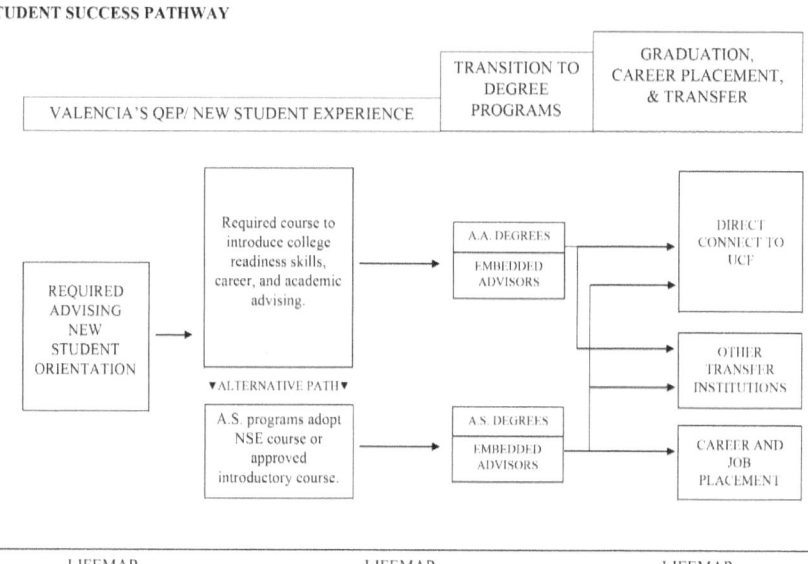

Figure 4.1. Student Success Pathway.

The college engaged in a collaborative design process with input from career center staff, academic advisors, deans, counselors, and faculty to infuse best practices in teaching and learning into the design of the advising program. The program focuses on students in specific career clusters with an emphasis on early career exploration at the front door.

Title V Grant Funding

In 2015, Valencia was awarded a Title V grant, which continued the work of the NSE. The work now focused on providing support to students after they had successfully completed fifteen credit hours but before completing forty-five hours and nearing graduation. The goals of the college's Title V grant were to:

- Enhance college infrastructure for increased engagement between students, faculty, and advisors.
- Increase student readiness for baccalaureate transfer by increasing capacity for advising through enhanced advising, new faculty roles, and technology.
- Strengthen data collection and analysis to reduce redundancy, increase efficiency, and support collaboration.

To effectively prepare students for transfer and allow them to fully leverage the DirectConnect to UCF partnership, advisors must be knowledgeable of specific academic program expectations at UCF. In an effort to increase communication and partnership between Valencia and UCF, focus groups and networking opportunities were coordinated for faculty and advisors across both institutions.

In addition to extensive conversations about course success indicators and program prerequisites, there were also discussions about nonacademic challenges that affect students' transfer experience. As a result, advising guides for specific baccalaureate majors were created that include academic, career, professional, and cocurricular guidelines as suggested milestones to help students toward degree completion. They also clearly delineate the roles and responsibilities of advisors and students.

STUDENTS' EXPERIENCE IN LIFEMAP 2.0

Valencia's LifeMap 2.0 model is based on five stages that addresses the needs of students from their entry into college to graduation and beyond:

college transition, introduction to college, progression to degree, graduation transition, and lifelong learning. The updated model is designed to provide students with a deeply personalized experience characterized by early connection and direction. Outreach to students is designed to be proactive throughout the students' time at the college, and advisors continue to play an active role throughout the student experience, treating the relationship as a partnership.

College Transition

The first LifeMap stage is defined by students' transition to college. In this stage, students are expected to engage fully in the enrollment process and make initial choices about educational and career interests (Romano, 2013). To support students in this stage, attendance at a new-student orientation is required of all new students, both first-time-in-college and transfer students, at Valencia.

New-Student Orientation

The new-student orientation model consists of a two-part orientation curriculum that includes student learning outcomes, active learning strategies, and assessment of student learning. Students complete the first part online, which includes information on degrees and meta-majors, as well as an informal career assessment. The module also includes information on Florida residency for tuition purposes and financial aid. The second part is a face-to-face experience that continues students' transition to college. The primary focus of the in-person orientation is to have all students engage in required academic advising to ensure that students are aware of gateway courses, register for courses in their first term, and engage in conversations with advisors about their intended major.

Introduction to College

The second LifeMap stage supports students during their first fifteen credit hours at the college. During their introduction to college, students are expected to complete a three-credit hour NSE course and develop an education plan that will guide course selection toward degree completion.

New Student Experience Course

Advising is embedded within the NSE course. The directors of advising established the advisor training curriculum for NSE faculty advisor training and continue to work with the faculty to further develop advising curriculum that is integrated within the training on how to teach the course. To support the success of NSE faculty advising, experienced advisors serve as mentors. This provides faculty with a named person they can reach out to whenever they have questions or come across more complicated advising scenarios. Advisor mentors also visit the classroom regularly to present on various topics. During the summer term, NSE faculty spend a majority of their time engaging with students through orientation, group advising, and meeting with students individually.

Progression to Degree

In the third LifeMap stage, students implement their educational plans and confirm or revisit decisions about their goals. Students in this stage typically have completed between sixteen and forty-four credit hours (Romano, 2013), and are supported by assigned advisors and proactive advising strategies.

Assignment to Program Advisors

All degree-seeking students are assigned to an advisor based on their intended educational pathway. Students pursuing an associate of science degree are assigned to a career program advisor when they first enroll at Valencia. Students who are pursuing an associate of arts degree are assigned to a program advisor after they complete twelve credit hours. Because all associate of arts degree students are required to take the NSE course within their first two terms, NSE faculty work collaboratively with advisors to support these students until they reach twelve credit hours. In working with either a career program advisor or program advisor, students experience the integration of career and academic advising. Both positions help to provide an advising system that identifies points of transition and struggle for students such as:

- Decisions about career and degree or major choice
- Pathways from course enrollment and degree completion
- From Valencia degree completion to bachelors or workplace

Proactive Advising Strategies

The LifeMap 2.0 model is characterized by a proactive advising communication plan that is timely, term and credit driven, and has intentional touch points. Communications sent to students are still primarily delivered through email, which can be a challenge because students tend to ignore emails. To counter the resistance to emails, advisors worked together to craft email language that is personalized, friendly, and includes graphics and pictures. To maintain consistency in communications, email templates were created by advisors and then shared with student focus groups for feedback on likability, tone, language, and clarity.

Some of the data points closely monitored by advisors include successful completion of common program prerequisites, grades in crucial courses, registration in rigorous classes, and lack of progression in sequential courses. Since the implementation of the communication plan, annual student engagement has increased by 47 percent, and more students are meeting with their advisors earlier in the registration period.

Certain student milestones have a long history at Valencia. New-student orientation, for example, has been a requirement for all degree-seeking students for well over twenty years. Students on academic probation and suspension also have been required to meet with an advisor. However, these milestones cannot be considered particularly proactive. As a broader vision of LifeMap 2.0, Valencia continues to explore what students should be required to experience and what should be optional learning opportunities. The Title III and V grants provided insight into required versus optional advising. Upcoming conversations and pilots will continue to help drive what will best serve student success.

Cocurricular Activities

Prior to the implementation of LifeMap 2.0, students' interactions with advisors were often limited to meeting advisors in their offices. Advisors are now much more involved in developing and implementing cocurricular activities based on established learning outcomes. These activities focus on promoting advising services, ensuring transfer readiness, and helping students explore majors and careers. Some of these initiatives include information sessions, career panels, open houses, major and transfer fairs, and professional networking events.

To increase students' career awareness and sense of academic purpose, an emphasis is placed on connecting students with alumni, employers, and industry professionals. The cocurricular activities have resulted in an increase in student engagement and stronger partnerships with faculty, the alumni office, internship and workforce opportunities, and the career center.

Graduation Transition

Once students complete forty-five credit hours, they enter the fourth LifeMap stage, during which they prepare for graduation. Assigned graduation advisors help support students who have entered this stage.

Graduation Advisors

To provide support to students regarding their graduation from Valencia, LifeMap 2.0 included the creation of a graduation advisor position. In this role, graduation advisors perform a comprehensive analysis of students' records to ensure that students are meeting their academic and degree requirements. The graduation advisors are proactive in their outreach once a student reaches forty-five credit hours to provide information about graduation planning, graduation application process, and to prompt students toward degree completion. Proactive outreach includes email and phone campaigns and on-campus workshops. Graduation advisors work closely with program advisors to review degree audits and monitor students' intended transfer institution plan. They also collaborate with related departments to maintain the accuracy of academic records and serve as points of contact for students, advisors, and the academic departments.

Lifelong Learning

The final LifeMap stage helps students develop an awareness that learning does not stop once a degree is earned. Students will be able to reengage the earlier LifeMap stages to set new goals, evaluate options, develop an education plan that meets additional learning needs, and follow their new educational plan at Valencia or other another institution (Romano, 2013).

SUPPORT FOR LIFEMAP

The implementation of LifeMap 2.0 required significant institutional investments, including additional staffing, professional development, and technology resources.

Staffing

Recommended advising caseloads can vary based on the institution size and type (Robbins, 2013). As recently as 2015, Valencia's student-to-advisor ratio was approximately 1,000:1. To help reduce the student-to-advisor ratio, the college followed a three-year implementation plan to hire fifty-two additional program advisors, resulting in the reduction of the student-to-advisor ratio to approximately 500:1, permitting advisors more opportunities to engage with students. To provide leadership and supervision to a significantly larger team of advisors, three Directors of Advising and five Assistant Directors of Advising were also hired, resulting in a total incremental staffing investment of about $2.9 million.

Professional Development

Valencia developed an advisor training curriculum that includes a historical overview of the college, the division's organizational structure, and information on services and resources available to students. It also includes an introduction to the National Academic Advising Association core values, ethics in advising, and a theoretical framework for the advising profession. Institution-specific information, such as academic policies and procedures, introduction to degrees, technical certificates, and majors is also included.

Career development is crucial to academic advising and therefore highly emphasized in the training. The advising curriculum also includes a focus on soft skills, which are essential to building personal connections with students. The onboarding training concludes with guided shadowing and reverse shadowing customized to each advisor's knowledge and experience in advising. A posttraining meeting is also scheduled by supervisors to discuss short- and long-term training goals.

Internal and External Partners

An essential element to the LifeMap 2.0 model focused on developing a stronger relationship between advisors and faculty. Since the onset of the model, the advisors regularly attend division meetings, which helps advisors stay updated on any curricular changes. As a result, faculty also have greater insight into services offered by student affairs. This increase in awareness provides an extra layer of support for students.

In the last few years, there has also been an increase in communication between Valencia and UCF advisors. Advisors schedule site visits to UCF, which has helped build relationships with advisors and administrators between the two colleges. Valencia advisors also attend curriculum-alignment meetings at UCF, which gives them a deeper knowledge of course expectations. Advisor participation in these UCF activities prepares them for more meaningful conversations with students.

Technology

To support the launch of LifeMap 2.0, the implementation of a customer relationship management (CRM) system was a focal point because it would allow for automation of many of the college's advising activities. However, the deployment of a CRM has been delayed, so other options were explored. In collaboration with Valencia's Institutional Research team, a statistical analysis systems (SAS) report was created for advisors so they could follow and monitor a student's progression.

The SAS report has been pivotal in the implementation of LifeMap 2.0 because it provides advisors with crucial data points about students' progression toward graduation. The work to identify and implement a CRM tool that will help accomplish the desired outcomes of LifeMap 2.0 continues. While research is in progress, advisors continue to be involved in the piloting of a CRM and provide crucially important feedback on the end-user experience.

While waiting for a CRM solution, the college also adopted an online appointment scheduling software to facilitate the process by which students make advising appointments. Because of the success of this appointment scheduling software pilot, other areas across the college implemented the scheduler, significantly increasing student access to meetings with advisors. The appointment scheduler provides an opportunity for technology to support the advisor-student partnership and improves data collection on their engagement.

Cycle of Assessment

Given that LifeMap 2.0 began in 2015, the data collected are relatively new. Data have been collected in three areas: student feedback, academic partnerships, and various quantitative measures. Students who have engaged with an advisor have completed surveys evaluating their experiences. Similarly, a survey captured feedback from academic departments to better understand the partnership with program advisors. Lastly, data continues to be collected on retention, persistence, course success, and other quantitative measures.

Student feedback has been particularly positive. When asked if their advisor appeared to have a genuine interest in helping, 87 percent of students responded "strongly agreed" and 9 percent "somewhat agreed." In responding to knowledge about their pathway to graduation, 97 percent responded they understood the number of credits and courses needed to graduate from Valencia. Additionally, 95 percent responded they understood the common program prerequisites needed for their baccalaureate degree. Seventy-two percent indicated they were following a term-by-term education plan they created. Comments from students also confirmed that students felt their advisors were helpful, caring, took extra time with them, and went "above and beyond" to resolve issues. Ninety-three percent of students surveyed also indicated they would recommend to other students that they meet with their advisors.

Advisors reported that students who are assigned to them have more insightful questions about educational pathways, are more knowledgeable about their program prerequisites, and are better prepared for appointments. Advisors attribute this change to the relationships they have been able to develop with their assigned students and having the ability to send students regular updates through email. Data tracking of student visits also shows that students are engaging with their advisors earlier in the term and not waiting until the last minute to register for upcoming classes.

Establishing relationships with the academic departments was essential to the success of the LifeMap 2.0 model. Academic deans were sent a survey to better understand and assess the strength of the partnership. The feedback was extremely positive and helped to reinforce the importance of the relationship between academic affairs and the program advisors. Within the survey, academic deans were given an opportunity to provide comments, and they agreed that faculty have a strong respect and appreciation for the advisors, "We treat them like they are part of the division . . . because they are." For the following responses, deans either, "strongly agreed" or "agreed" that program advisors:

- Communicated with them on a regular basis (100%)
- Contributed to departmental programming (94%)
- Regularly attended departmental meeting (94%)

Retention and persistence are other benchmarks that will be important to observe throughout the implementation of LifeMap 2.0. Institutional research at Valencia established a way to track students assigned to program advisors. Retention, persistence, withdrawal rates, grade point average, and course success rates are all indicators that will be monitored regularly. Within the first year of implementing LifeMap 2.0, persistence rates improved slightly. For the fall of 2016, a sample size of 1,367 students who met with their assigned advisors were tracked and 83.1 percent persisted to the next term, compared to only 80.6 percent (1,595) of students who had not met with an advisor, persisting to their next term.

In reviewing data from the 2017–2018 academic year, there was a difference in withdrawal and success rates when comparing students who met with an advisor to those who did not meet with an advisor. Withdrawal rates for students who saw an advisor was 8.8 percent compared with 10.6 percent for those who did not meet with an advisor. When reviewing success rates, which is defined as, "students receiving grades of A, B, or C," 80.7 percent of students who met with an advisor were successful compared with 76.3 percent who did not meet with an advisor.

Although data are not extensive, it will be imperative to keep track of these quantitative measures to explore ways that LifeMap 2.0 might influence student success. Future assessments will include examining the number of students who complete program prerequisites prior to graduation and transfer. Advising strategies will also be evaluated to determine how they might contribute to closing the achievement gaps for underserved students.

As Valencia assesses the effects of LifeMap 2.0, the college's focus must not be on how Valencia experiences its students, but rather how students experience Valencia (Shugart, Phelps, Puyana, Romano, & Walter, n.d.). Valencia has a deep history of not seeing students as enrollment numbers, but as individual human beings with distinct gifts, talents, and callings. The college has been challenged to maintain its ability to serve students in a deeply personalized way, and LifeMap 2.0 has allowed Valencia to respond to challenges in a manner consistent with this philosophy. Valencia looks forward to the evolution of LifeMap 2.0, and the resulting positive influence on its students and the community it serves.

REFERENCES

Cho, S. W., & Karp, M. M. (2013). Student success courses in the community college: Early enrollment and educational outcomes. *Community College Review, 41*(1), 86–103.

Frost, S. (1991) *Academic advising for student success: A system of shared responsibility.* Washington, DC: ASHE-ERIC Higher Education Reports. Retrieved from ERIC database. (ED340274)

Klingman, P. D. (2008). Encouraging Dialogue and Consensus Building (1995–1998). In B. Castellano & S. Kelley (Eds.), *Valencia Community College: A history of an extraordinary learning community.* Orlando, FL: Valencia Community College.

Math Pathways. (n.d.) Retrieved from http://catalog.valenciacollege.edu/entrytesting-placementmandatorycourses/testingplacementcharts/Math_Pathways_Chart_Final.pdf

O'Banion, T. (1997). *A learning college for the 21st century.* Phoenix, AZ: Oryx Press.

Romano, J. (2013). Valencia College: A learning-centered student advising system. In T. O'Banion (Ed.), *Academic advising: The key to student success* (pp. 33–56). Washington, DC: Community College Press.

Robbins, R. (2013). Advisor load. Retrieved from https://www.nacada.ksu.edu/Resources/Clearinghouse/View-Articles/Advisor-Load.aspx

Scott-Clayton, J. (2011). The shapeless river: Does a lack of structure inhibit students' progress at community college? (CRCC Working Paper No. 25). Community College Research Center: Columbia University.

Shugart, S. (2014, October 17). *Collaboration as an architectural metaphor* [Video file]. Retrieved from https://www.youtube.com/watch?v=tQC03CutwcA

Shugart, S. C. (2016). Why higher education? Lessons learned in a learner-centered college. *New Directions for Teaching and Learning, 145,* 85–91.

Shugart, S., & Romano, J. C. (2006). LifeMap: A learning-centered system for student success. *Community College Journal of Research and Practice, 30*(2), 141–143.

Shugart, S. C., Phelps, J., Puyana, A., Romano, J., & Walter, K. (n.d.). Valencia's big ideas: Sustaining authentic organizational change through shared purpose and culture. Retrieved from https://valenciacollege.edu/about/trustee-education/documents/big-ideas-trustees.pdf

UCF Office of Institutional Research. (2016). *UCF Florida College System consortium partners' student success feedback report: Valencia College 2015–2016.* Orlando, FL: University of Central Florida.

FIVE
Flight of the Hawks

A Pathways Approach to Advising

Sheryl Otto and Victoria Atkinson

> "I know I will succeed in college . . . because I want a better life for myself and for my family . . . and Harper College was the right choice for me."
>
> (Anonymous student, Summer 2018)

The community college hallmarks of open access and freedom to use services as needed assume a level of self-directedness that twenty-first-century students may not possess. They display vulnerability in terms of goals and indecision, often lack financial support, and are increasingly the first generation of their family to attend college. These factors result in a call to action to move away from long menus of options and replace them with more focused and integrated student experiences.

Advising is intended to directly and positively influence student success, and, for this to occur, old models of academic advising are in need of significant reform. The movement away from a la carte models and menus of services and progress toward intentional, focused, and clearly articulated goals is a complex process for any institution to undertake.

William Rainey Harper College (Harper College) in Palatine, Illinois, began a journey of reform in 2009 with the arrival of President Kenneth Ender. During the last ten years, Harper College's strategic focus on student success has become more prominent and reflects the nationwide emphasis on completion. Harper College is a comprehensive community college located in northwest suburban Chicago that celebrated its fiftieth anniversary in 2017. It serves approximately 15,000 credit students annually in associate degree and certificate programs. The student population is increasingly diverse, a reflection of the changing demographics in the local community.

Harper College boasts a long-standing tradition of focusing on student success. As an early adopter of mandatory placement testing, advising, and new-student orientation, it embraced the burgeoning "first year" movement in the 1990s and added courses and programs to support students in transition. Dating back to the late 1960s, the advising model at Harper College included full- and part-time professional counselors with master's degrees who provided holistic advising in decentralized centers across campus. The full-time counselors held nine-month, tenured positions and, although they worked in various locations across campus, they united through a common mission and reported to the dean of Student Development. This model had many strengths and was recognized as an exemplary program in *Academic Advising: The Key to Student Success* (O'Banion, 2013). But even exemplary programs must adapt to changing times to remain proactive, effective, and achieve outcomes-based excellence.

Responding to concerns identified by thought leaders, Harper College began to examine its practices and gaps related to supporting student success and completion. This included reflection on the poor completion rates for community college students; as many as 50 percent of entering students fell prey to attrition in their first year (Crane, 2008). Harper College was called to action in part by President Obama's American Graduation Initiative, which laid out a vision of five million additional community college graduates by 2020. Harper College embraced this challenge and identified its proportional share, 10,604, which became a unifying completion goal across campus.

Through its involvement with Achieving the Dream, Harper College began a thorough, data-informed examination of its record on student outcomes. In 2010, the college launched a five-year strategic plan requiring comprehensive reform to increase completion by supporting all students in addressing their individual needs and closing achievement gaps between the average Harper College student and underperforming students. This strategic plan resulted in the establishment of a program in which faculty, early in the semester, identified first-year students struggling in the classroom and referred them to counselors for assistance. This early alert program was the first significant initiative that began to transform the academic advising model.

At that time, students were not assigned to specific counselors for academic advising. Except for students on academic probation, they were not required to meet with a counselor for educational planning once they completed the mandatory new-student orientation. With the adoption of the early alert program, each new student flagged for concern was assigned to a specific counselor to create a team of support consisting of the counselor, academic faculty, and student. As part of this team effort, it was expected that the counselors would follow each student through the completion of the first year, although no consistent guidelines defined how counselors were to do this task.

The early alert program proved to be effective, increasing both student persistence and successful course completion rates. However, the program was limited to several hundred students, and the counselor-to-student ratios were too high to support rapid growth of the program. During this time, Harper College began to move away from boutique programs that served subsets of students and explored how effective programs could be expanded ("scaling up"). This thinking led to the next proposal that changed the advising model.

A strategic initiative involving academic success coaches was designed to be more proactive and intrusive with students, leveraging insights gleaned from early alert that the relationship with a particular support person was pivotal. The goal was to determine a way to assign all credential-seeking students to an advocate who would serve as a consistent point of contact to assist the student in navigating the Harper College experience.

To pilot this concept, three academic success coaches were hired. The individuals carried a caseload of students, served as resource experts, and helped students strengthen self-advocacy skills. Although theoretically a good idea, students were confused about how the roles of counselors and success coaches were different, and success coaches' lack of academic advising training limited their ability to fully help the students.

In September of 2016, Harper College held a full-day retreat with twenty-five administrators, faculty, and staff to identify a sustainable structure to ensure that all students were assigned an advocate from start to finish. The goal of the advocate would be to make sure that every student pursuing a credential would create an education and career plan that led to completion. A task force formed to develop a job description for twelve-month, bachelor-level (master's preferred) academic advisors.

During this time, Harper College adopted its second strategic plan under President Ender, influenced heavily by *Redesigning America's Community Colleges: A Clearer Path to Student Success* (Bailey, Jaggars, & Jenkins, 2015). Many staff and faculty began following the Community College Research Center's (CCRC) work and noted the importance of avoiding the "shapeless river" (Scott-Clayton, 2011). College leaders came to understand that too many choices for students can lead to decision fatigue and paralysis, but Harper College had not integrated those concerns fully into its structure. A renewed focus developed on the importance of having an intentional, consistent experience for all students, with an emphasis on early identification of career goals through a unified "pathways" approach.

Harper College formed ten academic areas of interest to simplify how prospective students explore its offerings. The areas of interest (listed at the bottom of Figure 5.1) also create a framework in which students, faculty, and staff can communicate and foster a sense of mutual support and belonging. As the new advising model came into focus, the need to align it with the areas of interest guided pathways structure became clear. The conceptual model evolved to link each advisor with two areas of interest and assign students to an advisor primarily by students' program of study.

As the creation of Harper College's guided pathways approach continued, the campus community organized and restructured various services, programs, and functions. Momentum built, but gaps existed because of inconsistent adoption of the new guided pathways concepts and language. Harper College lacked a conceptual model to clearly articulate the goals and intentions of these purposeful efforts. As a result, the creation of a framing paradigm of crucial student lifecycle activities for all credential-seeking students, inclusive of the many cross-institutional student success efforts, began to emerge. Titled "Flight of the Hawks" after Harper College's mascot, this concept map was rooted in Completion by Design's (2016) Loss-Momentum Framework and concepts from Achieving the Dream and CCRC.

Flight of the Hawks identified four main stages using the construct of SOAR: *Search* (Explore Your Journey); *Onboard* (Prepare to Take Flight); *Advance* (Follow Your Flight Plan); and *Realize* (Ensure a Successful Landing). Essential components of the student journey identified include:

- Exploring career options and choosing a program of study early
- Developing a personalized plan to completion with the assigned advisor
- Engaging with faculty, staff, and the wide array of support services to make steady progress and build essential skills
- Earning a credential, joining the Harper College network of alumni, and going forward toward career advancement or further education

Flight of the Hawks and the SOAR framework provided a common language to describe the Harper College experience expected for all credential-seeking students. As the new advising model came into focus, its adoption and use became essential organizing constructs with advisors playing a primary role in guiding students through this journey map.

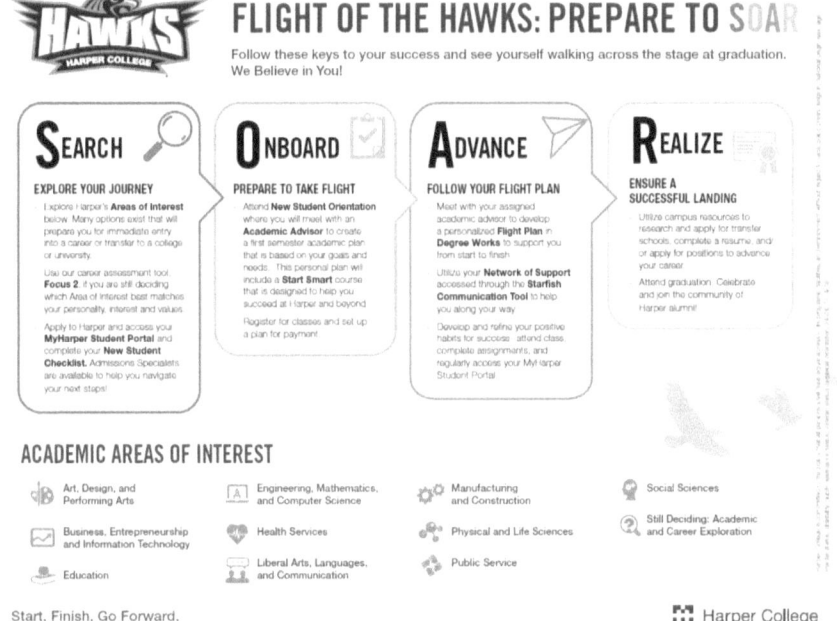

Figure 5.1.

The revised case management advising model launched in the summer of 2017 with a goal of assigning 3,000 students in the initial year. Nineteen existing positions on campus were restructured into an academic advisor role, and funding was allocated to hire additional academic advisors. The advisors completed training and began meeting with students during orientation to build their caseloads.

Initial caseload sizes were approximately 150 with the expectation as the program continued to scale that caseload sizes would grow to approximately 250–350 enrolled students per advisor. In two years, the program has grown to thirty-three full-time advisors with more than 7,500 students assigned for an average caseload of approximately 227. Initially, the counselors also carried caseloads and provided academic advising, but they no longer do so. Counselor roles have since been recrafted to complement academic advising by providing academic, career, and personal counseling.

In the new model, both academic advisors and counselors report to the Student Development Division, which has a unified vision and mission of holistic student support. To aid the dean of Student Development in running the new case-management advising model, four managerial positions were created through restructuring: associate dean of Advising Services, manager of Advising and Counseling Operations, and two lead advisors. All play an essential role in ensuring that an appropriate infrastructure is in place with technological resources, case management guidelines, advisor training and development, and assessment plans so that the program continues to thrive as it matures.

PATHWAYS ADVISING UNDER THE SOAR FRAMEWORK

Every component of the case management advising model was designed to successfully move students through their SOAR flight path. From start to finish, the academic advisor serves as a co-pilot with the student on this journey. The SOAR framework provides a meaningful way to describe the advising model in further detail.

During the Search stage, students are directed to:

- Explore and choose one of ten academic areas of interest and consider a pathway that leads to transferring to a university or immediate employment.
- Apply to Harper College.

SEARCH

EXPLORE YOUR JOURNEY

Figure 5.2.

- Submit the Free Application for Federal Student Aid.
- Access their MyHarper Portal dashboard and complete their personalized New Student Checklist.

Although staff in Admissions Outreach and the one-stop enrollment center provide primary support to prospective students, academic advisors assist as needed, especially with prospective students who want early assistance with career decision making. Career counseling and exploration services previously offered in a separate center on campus were intentionally reframed and integrated within the new student onboarding process. Using Focus 2 Career, an online career interest and exploration tool available on Harper College's website and embedded within the areas of interest, prospective students explore how their interests, skills, and personality align with careers before orientation and initial advising. Focus 2 Career results are customized to Harper's academic offerings to assist in narrowing career choices.

During the *Onboard* stage, students are directed to:

- Complete their orientation.
- Meet their advisor, who will help them navigate from start to graduation.
- Complete their first-semester academic plan with their advisor.
- Register for classes, including a Start Smart course aligned by areas of interest
- Set up a financial plan for payment.

New-Student Orientation and Onboarding

Through MyHarper Portal, students have 24/7 access to essential new student information, including an online introduction to orientation em-

ONBOARD
PREPARE TO TAKE FLIGHT

Figure 5.3.

bedded in the New Student Checklist. This informative introduction is a preview to the mandatory in-person orientation. The online preview sets the stage for the Flight of the Hawks student journey, providing a high-level overview of SOAR and expectations. The importance of in-person orientation is explained to students as the opportunity to meet their advisor to help them personalize their plan and set the stage for success.

Included in the on-campus orientation experience are opportunities to meet current students. Student orientation leaders are hired specifically to reflect the diverse campus community in terms of age, ethnicity, and educational goals. Students are offered "tours on demand" at any time to provide a customized campus overview, inclusive of resources and services for success. Parking tips and campus navigation are popular requests, along with directions to the Starbucks on campus.

Within MyHarper Portal, students access Starfish by Hobsons, Harper College's chosen communication tool to support the case-management model. Students complete a customized "student intake" in Starfish, which allows advisors, prior to initial advising, to learn more about students' concerns. In summer 2018, advisors learned the following insights about their students:

- 18 percent planned to work more than twenty-five hours per week.
- 25 percent indicated slight or no confidence in study skills.
- 25 percent indicated slight or no confidence in time-management skills.
- 46 percent expressed concerns about how to pay for school.
- 83 percent indicated certainty about career goals.

This input from students, prior to the one-on-one advising, provides advisors with an opportunity to address concerns and provides students with an opportunity to acknowledge factors that may inhibit their success.

In addition, an open-ended "getting to know you" statement is included in the intake: *I know I will succeed in college because. . . .* Sample responses to the statement include:

"I am hard working and I want to be better to provide for my family."

"I know I'll have a support system to guide me through college."

"I trust in this school and those who work here."

The results serve as powerful reminders of the importance of advisors adopting a growth mindset (Dweck, 2006) to empower students and challenge them to work hard to achieve their goals, while offering support.

Taking Off: The Academic Flight Plan

The key outcome of advising in the *Onboard* stage is the first semester of an academic "flight plan" that is stored electronically in Ellucian Degree Works. To create the personalized first semester plan, advisors assess students' levels of college readiness through a careful review of high school transcripts, prior college credit (if any), standardized test results, and local placement test results.

Students who place at the developmental level are guided to enroll in mandatory courses in English, math, or both. Advisors are better able to map a student's path to completion within their area of interest when necessary courses, such as math, are clearly explained in relationship to academic goals. Similarly, students are guided to enroll in one of many Start Smart first-year experience courses, which are tailored to areas of interest with campus engagement and success strategies. Students who are undecided are encouraged to enroll in a *Focus on Your Future* Start Smart course designed specifically to support career exploration and goal setting. These Start Smart courses stress the importance of students connecting with their academic advisor to build their educational plan to completion.

As students transition from *Onboard* to *Advance*, the student-advisor assignment is made. Four primary factors are used in making the assignments:

- Preserving continuity, as much as possible, with the advisor the student met at orientation
- Advisor caseload size (having balance among advisors)

- Student's intended area of interest
- Student's connection to a specialized advising population, if applicable

Each advisor is affiliated with two areas of interest to become more expert in the nuances and specifics of affiliated programs of study; however, it has not been possible to use that as a rigid assignment criterion. First, great variation exists in the number of students pursuing the different degrees and certificates, so using that factor alone results in vastly differing caseload sizes across advisors. Second, students occasionally change their minds about their intended academic program. Preserving the *relationship* aspect of the case management advising model is an essential principle. That purpose is defeated if the advisor is changed every time the student changes programs. Therefore, advisors are trained as generalists and provide academic planning for all Harper College programs and transfer pathways.

Although time-consuming and imperfect, the assignment process works. Early concerns about the chaos that might ensue to rematch students to new advisors related to goals, student characteristics, and personalities were unfounded, even in the first rollout of the process in 2017. More than anything, students listened to Harper College's promise to provide an expert advisor to guide them on their "flight." And with more than 3,000 students assigned that fall, fewer than 2 percent of students requested a change to another advisor.

During the Advance stage, students are directed to:

- Meet with their assigned academic advisor to finish developing their personalized academic flight plan.
- Use their network of support (faculty, academic advisor, and academic support) to help them along their way.

Figure 5.4.

- Develop and refine their positive habits for success—attend class, engage with faculty, complete assignments, and regularly access their MyHarper Portal.

Following the Academic Flight Plan

At orientation, only the first semester of the academic flight plan is created. During the first semester, there is an expectation that students will build the remainder of their plan with their advisor through enrollment in a Start Smart first-year experience course. Developing the semester-by-semester outline of the courses needed to meet each student's intended goal is a learning outcome of the course. Once built, the primary emphasis is the need for students to continue to meet with their advisor to keep their academic flight plan up-to-date. This is especially important as students make adjustments to their goals such as selecting a new major, changing their transfer school destination, or moving from full-time to part-time enrollment.

To have the student's academic flight plan accessible and visible, considerable time and effort went into integrating and customizing supporting technology tools. Ellucian Degree Works is used by the advisors and students for the electronic storage of the student's plan. In addition to the semester-by-semester academic flight plan in Degree Works, students and advisors are able to run degree audits. The audit is a comparison of the courses a student has taken toward a particular degree or certificate. The student's coursework can be audited against any program Harper College offers and provides helpful insights as a student considers a potential change in direction or an additional credential.

Students access Degree Works through MyHarper Portal. Of significance is a customization made to the MyHarper Portal that provides students with a quick and easy visual progress check each time they log in.

Students see a horizontal progress bar that shows their completion percentage based on the number of credit hours and requirements earned toward the intended credential. Additionally, they see their assigned advisor's name, academic flight plan title, program of study, and status indicating whether they are on or off track for their plan based on the courses in which they are enrolled. Providing students with real-time visuals about their progress serves as encouragement and promotes personal accountability, especially if off track.

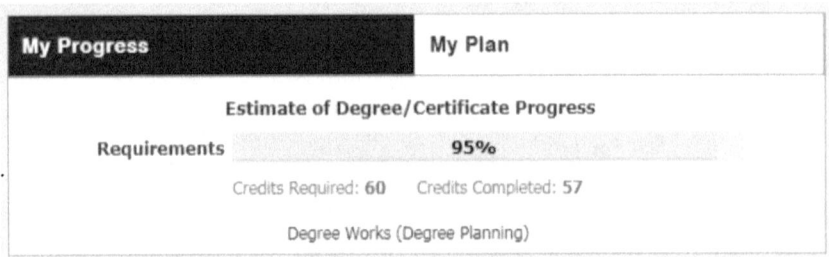

Figure 5.5.

A further point of integration between electronic academic planning tools is the connection between Degree Works and College Scheduler by Civitas Learning. As students prepare to register, they can use College Scheduler to streamline the process. The student's courses from Degree Works show in College Scheduler, and the student can seamlessly select those courses for the upcoming term. When using College Scheduler, if the student attempts to schedule something other than what is on plan, a warning is prompted. Additionally, students can identify the days of week and times of day with potential conflicts due to work, family, or other commitments. College Scheduler presents students with enrollment options to meet academic and work–life balance needs.

Network of Support

The assigned advisor is the student's point person for navigating the Harper College experience from start to finish, but there are others who play an influential role in student success, including faculty and support service staff. Providing coordinated and holistic assistance is a key feature of the case-management model.

Case-management guidelines and reports provide direction, continuity, and quality standards. With more than thirty advisors, it is important that they work as a unified whole to maximize effect and ensure consistency in the student experience. The case-management guidelines outline expectations for all advisors and establish the minimum number of contacts needed with caseloads. See Table 5.1 for examples of standard emails sent.

These advisor-led outreach efforts are incorporated into the overall student communication plan each year to minimize duplication in mes-

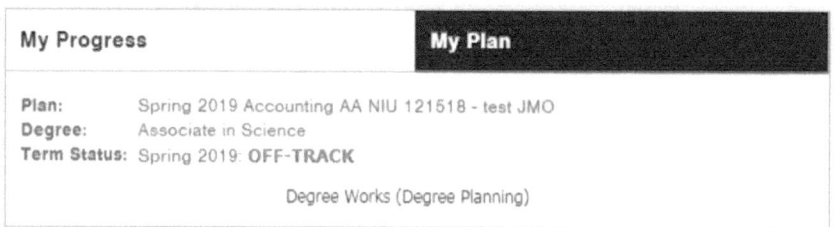

Figure 5.6.

saging from other parts of Harper College. As advisors build relationships with their students, they are encouraged to send additional personalized messages with tips, reminders, and encouragement. To aid the advisors with tracking their students and developing those individualized communications, each week they receive a report that summarizes students' progress on key metrics. Advisors can drill down into the report to get lists of students who need additional attention, such as those who have not registered for the upcoming semester or those who are off track with their plan.

Harper College uses Starfish as the communication tool that connects students, advisors, faculty, and other support staff. Via Starfish, advisors send students emails and make notes about interactions and outreach efforts. Students access Starfish through the MyHarper Portal. Their support network is viewable for the semester including contact information for their assigned advisor, instructors, and Tutoring Center personnel. Starfish allows emails to be sent and received within their network.

Additionally, Starfish is used as an early alert tool. During week 4 and week 10 of the semester, faculty receive electronic surveys asking them about the progress of students with at-risk or high-stakes characteristics. Faculty can provide notes of concern or encouragement (kudos) that the student and assigned advisor also see. When concerns are raised, the advisor, instructor, and student connect to develop a success plan for the particular course.

Starfish is also used as a referral hub. For example, faculty can suggest that students attend tutoring. Staff in the Tutoring Center receive that referral and provide additional outreach to the student. Counselors are also connected within Starfish to the academic advisors. When advisors encounter students who need career, academic, or personal counseling,

Table 5.1. Consistent Advisor Email Outreaches Per Semester

Timing	Topic
Week 2	Welcome—whether new student, new to caseload, or starting a new semester
Week 4	Academic Flight Plan—for new students, to get it created; for continuing students, how to update and follow it
Week 6	Midterm Progress Check—promotion of support services and success tips
Week 9/10	Preparing for Next Semester—registration or graduation information

they send a referral through Starfish. Regardless of the circumstances, advisors are always encouraged to "close the loop" and provide the appropriate level of feedback, protecting student privacy where warranted, to instructors and other support staff about their follow-up interactions as a result of referrals.

The areas of interest core teams, consisting of advisors, faculty, counselors, and other support staff, as needed, further enhance communication and promote student success. The core teams meet to discuss curricular changes, ways to support student success, and opportunities for additional partnerships. Microsoft team sites have been created to support online partnership and document sharing to ensure advising accuracy.

Specialized Advising

Although Flight of the Hawks lays the foundation for a consistent experience for all credential-seeking students, that level of support is not sufficient to address the needs or achievement gaps of every student. Identification of groups of students needing additional or specialized assistance occurs through various data-informed means. Analysis of information secured through Harper College's involvement with Achieving the Dream identified students with large achievement gaps, primarily students placed in developmental coursework upon entry and African American males. National and local data point to the need for added support and intervention for other populations:

- Underserved and underrepresented populations such as single parents; students with disabilities; and students who are low income, first generation, and nonnative speakers
- Students on academic and financial aid probation, along with those having moderate, low, and very low persistence rankings identified by Civitas Learning's predictive analytics
- High-stakes students who, although they may not be listed as at-risk, need special monitoring to ensure their success; athletes and students enrolled in a challenging engineering baccalaureate transfer pathway are examples

The case management advising model provides supplemental support to these special populations. First, attributes in Starfish allow advisors to filter and sort their caseload among a variety of characteristics that include race and ethnicity, first-generation college status, whether a student is registered for the current or upcoming semester, and whether the student has an academic flight plan for an upcoming term. Academic advisors sort by one or more of these attributes to check on the progress of a subset of their caseload or send a customized message to a particular group. Second, twenty-six of the advisors are generalists aligned by areas of interest, and seven are specialized advisors who work with a specific population of students. Examples of differentiated advising support based on student type include the following:

- The Rita and John Canning Women's Program consists of three advisors who provide educational planning and financial support for low-income individuals who also meet eligibility criteria.
- In partnership with the nonprofit organization *One Million Degrees*, Harper College provides wrap-around services (academic advising, tutoring, coaching, financial support, and success workshops) for low-income, highly motivated students, many of whom are first-generation or racially or ethnically diverse. The program is staffed by two academic advisors and one director who carries a small caseload.
- One academic advisor is devoted to working with students who speak English as a second language (ESL). This advisor provides guidance and support to students enrolled in ESL coursework. The ESL advisor helps students who progress to credential-seeking programs to make that transition, at which point the student is as-

signed a new advisor to help navigate the remainder of the Harper College experience.
- Students on academic probation must meet with an academic advisor to develop a success plan before being permitted to enroll in the subsequent semester.
- Access and Disability Services (ADS) provides students with legally mandated accommodations and other programming to promote the inclusion and success of students with disabilities. In addition to the assigned academic advisor, each student who registers with ADS is assigned an access advocate. The advisor and advocate work closely to ensure that the student's accommodation plan and academic plan align.

The *Realize* stage focuses on ensuring students have a successful landing and are prepared for their next step after Harper College. Students should:

- Use campus resources to research and apply for transfer schools, complete a resume, and apply for positions to advance their career.
- Attend graduation and celebrate.
- Join the community of Harper College alumni.

Use Campus Resources

MyHarper Portal serves as students' centralized hub for personal and general information. Providing students with 24/7 access promotes their own accountability in their Harper College experience and empowers them with the information and tools needed to be successful.

There are seven categories of resources in the MyHarper Portal:

- My Profile

Figure 5.7.

- Academic Advising and Counseling
- Registration and Records
- Finances
- Student Life
- Academic Success
- Job Resources

Within the Academic Advising and Counseling section, students access their academic flight plan and assigned advisor. Additionally, they access resources to assist in transferring to baccalaureate programs offered on campus through the University Center. Resources are also provided for career and personal counseling, including the Focus 2 Career tool, which can be taken repeatedly to allow students to explore options and alternatives with linkages to career and labor market information. Timely tips rotate throughout the academic year reminding students about important deadlines and promoting events such as visits by four-year college representatives and employers.

A full complement of workshops on advising, counseling, and student success topics have been developed, which faculty can request to be presented in the classroom. Advisors also created a "street team" to bring programs and services to areas where students gather outside of class. The street team programs are themed with an outcome that corresponds to the SOAR framework and are delivered in conjunction with other offices, such as One Stop, Student Involvement, and Success Services.

The other sections of MyHarper Portal provide students with similar information and tools to ensure they are making the most of their Harper College experience. Student Life promotes clubs, organizations, campus events, and other engagement opportunities; Academic Success focuses on resources provided by the Tutoring Center, Writing Center, and Access and Disability Services; and Job Resources highlights the services offered by the Job Placement Resource Center that includes résumé creation and review, interviewing practice, internships and co-ops search, job search, and on-campus employment for student aides.

Graduation and Beyond

With a strategic focus on student success and completion, graduation is a celebrated tradition. The case management advising model, inclusive of early alert, helped Harper College surpass the goal in 2017 of graduating 10,604 *additional* students by 2020. A new outdoor pavilion serves as the on-campus graduation site. Students, families, faculty, and staff actively join in the celebration. As anticipated, many advisors and students form close bonds. Advisors take pride in attending the ceremony and celebrating their students' accomplishments. Students who return to Harper College for another credential know whom to contact for help.

Although completion of the degree or certificate is the aspirational goal, for certain students that isn't practical or possible. For a variety of reasons, some students leave Harper College without a credential. Prior to the case-management advising model, there was no systemic outreach to such students, nor was Harper College aware of why the student may have left. Now, advisors are able to record leaving notes in Starfish. The institution is able to examine that data in aggregate to better understand the reasons for attrition and develop supports to offset those causes. Additionally, these stop-out students remain in an advisor's caseload for up to three semesters. Advisors do periodic outreach to stop-out students to provide assistance whenever they are ready to resume studies.

EVALUATION AND EFFECT

With an institutional culture of assessment and data-informed decision-making, multiple measures are employed to provide both formative and summative evaluation of the case-management advising model. Conducting this research is a team effort, and relies on expertise from the Institutional Research and Information Technology departments. As part of the integration of the multiple technologies supporting the model, essential data elements contained within those systems were added to the institutional reporting and data warehouse. This has been crucial to create reports that provide insights into progress both real time and over time.

Caseload Size and Penetration Rate

A weekly audit report lists each counselor's caseload size and the names of assigned students. This report ensures that caseloads remain as balanced as possible across advisors and is helpful if students need to be reassigned either on a permanent or temporary basis. This report also identifies progress toward reaching scale, defined as the assignment of every credential-seeking student to an academic advisor. To date, over 7,500 students have been assigned which represents 71 percent of credential-seeking students.

Usage and Engagement Rates

On-demand reports show student usage of advising including total number and type of appointments, no shows, and reschedules. These reports assist in tracking volume patterns.

Advisors receive a weekly report with essential information about their students that prioritizes who needs additional intervention. The first page of the report provides summary information including the number and percentage of students with an academic flight plan, registered for the upcoming semester, with a future appointment scheduled, and with a leaving note. Advisors drill down to specific lists of students associated with those activities. As an example, the list of students without an academic flight plan includes names, identification numbers, contact information, program of study, hours earned, grade point average, and date of last advising appointment. Advisors can also retrieve a list of students who are off-track with their academic flight plan that contains information about the specific courses that are causing the student to be off plan.

Supervisors receive a comparable weekly summary report of critical success metrics to monitor individual and collective progress. These combined efforts yielded impressive results. Figure 5.8 demonstrates the growth in student use of advising and the creation of an academic flight plan during the first semester prior to the case managed model and after.

Retention and Graduation Rates

Fall-to-spring and fall-to-fall persistence rates are tracked. Given the early stages of the model, more data currently exist for fall-to-spring persistence rates. Institutional fall-to-spring persistence rates increased by three percentage points since the implementation of the case-management advising model. Fall-to-spring persistence rates for students with an assigned advisor are 14 percentage points higher than for students without an assigned advisor (77 percent vs. 63 percent). As shown in Figure 5.9, students who follow through and meet with their advisor

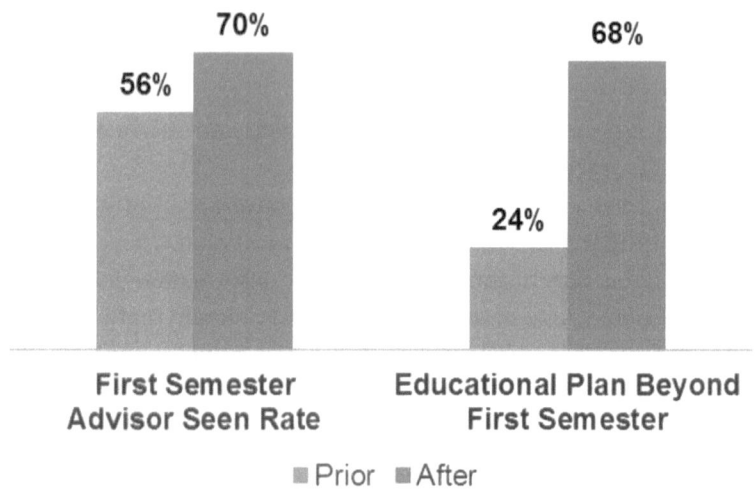

Figure 5.8.

have higher persistence rates than those who do not meet with their advisor.

Having an academic flight plan also results in a retention boost. In fall 2018, 94 percent of new, degree-seeking students who are in college for the first time and have a plan returned for the spring semester, whereas only 59 percent of those without a plan returned. Harper College achieved a three-year graduation rate of 32.7 percent, an increase of 11 percentage points since 2014, and the highest rate in Harper College's recorded history attributable to a number of coordinated strategic initiatives in which the redesign of advising played a major role.

Constituent Feedback

In addition to the Community College Survey of Student Engagement, which is administered every three years, annual point-of-service surveys collect data about students' satisfaction with their advising experience. Students positively rate their experiences with their academic advisors. In evaluations gathered in fall 2018, advisors' overall satisfaction

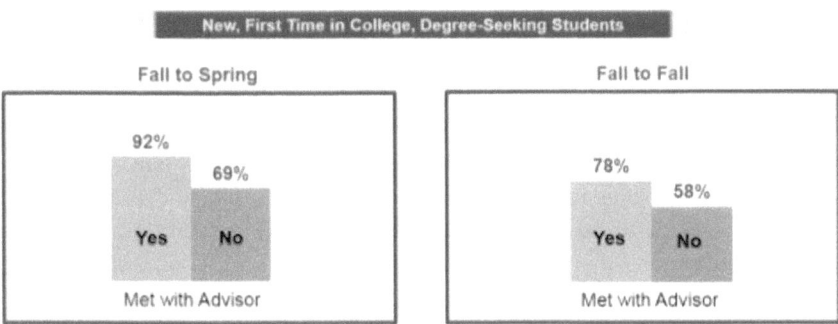

Figure 5.9.

ratings ("strongly agree") were at 90 percent or higher for each of the following statements:

- My advisor was welcoming.
- My advisor motivated me.
- My advisor knew about my major, program of study, area of interest, and academic goals.
- My advisor reviewed my audit with me.
- My advisor asked me if I had questions about my plan.

Equally important is the feedback from students as a result of new-student orientation and initial advising. Results gathered from summer 2018 show 90 percent or higher strong agreement with the following statements:

- I felt welcomed at orientation.
- I understand how Focus 2 Career and Degree Works will help me be successful at Harper.
- As a result of the Flight of the Hawks SOAR plan discussed in orientation, I feel more confident about being a student at Harper.
- I know it will be important to meet with my advisor in the future to stay on track and complete my goals.

During regularly scheduled case management meetings that all advisors attend, opportunities to showcase successes and to problem-solve challenges occur. This feedback is invaluable for continuous improvement. Additionally, the associate dean of Advising Services, as part of her doctoral dissertation (Hoffhines, 2018), evaluated the effect of strategies within the case-management advising model. Two student focus groups and one advisor focus group were conducted. The following themes emerged:

Overall students were able to articulate how the assigned advisor relationship was making a difference. Said one student,

> I think it feels very warm and comforting to know that you have someone who's involved in your education other than a parent a guardian or yourself. So, to be having someone like that at school also makes you want to expand that kind of feeling into other places. You're like oh, I'm comfortable here, I might as well join a club; I'm comfortable here, I can talk more in class. Like it definitely has an effect I've noticed.

Results from the focus groups and advisor input led to the refinement of the case-management guidelines, enhancements to data collection and reports, suggestions for streamlining technology tools, and further professional development and training.

As an important stakeholder, faculty feedback sessions were conducted to gather input and suggestions for improvement on early alert. Typically, more than five hundred faculty receive at least one early alert survey each semester. Although response rates have been strong, averaging around 70 percent as the program has scaled, faculty participation has declined slightly. Ensuring that faculty remain informed and invested in this effort is essential to its success. After gathering input from both faculty and advisors, more than thirty-five enhancements were made to the early alert and Starfish systems.

Faculty also provided input on ways to tailor the onboarding experience for students based on areas of interest. Areas of interest listening sessions were conducted, with more than sixty faculty attending. This feedback will directly shape content for the revised pathways approach to new-student orientation beginning summer 2019.

Table 5.2. Case Management Strategies

Student Theme Summary	Advisor Theme Summary
• The academic flight plan helps students visualize their future. • Proactive communication by the advisor is helpful.	• Technology use during appointments can detract from rapport building and may overwhelm some students. • Proactive communication is more effective when tailored to individual advisees. • Students need extra encouragement to seek support services.

TRAINING AND PROFESSIONAL DEVELOPMENT

A comprehensive training program exists for the thirty-three academic advisors and is overseen by the associate dean of Advising Services along with support from the lead advisors. Components of the training program include:

- Philosophical grounding in the principles of developmental advising and growth mindset
- Expectations of the case-management approach
- Descriptions of college and external resources
- Instruction in the mechanics of academic advising, including the use of technology for electronic educational plans and notes, student appointment management, and early alert

Ongoing professional development is provided for the academic advisors on a variety of topics, including program and curriculum updates, understanding the diverse nature of students, and more.

As Flight of the Hawks becomes more embedded, the importance of providing support to new advisors is essential. In addition to learning about Harper College programs and services, new team members are expected to adopt a wholehearted embrace of the tenets foundational to the Flight of the Hawks model. The focus on equity, access, wrap-around support, and service must drive decisionmaking, use of time, and professional development efforts. To that end, new advisors are mentored by a seasoned advising colleague to provide easy access to information and support. Nurturing the model and the players who embody it matters, almost as much as the model itself.

A PERSONAL PERSPECTIVE

Although many factors contributed to the successful advising redesign at Harper College, two foundational elements were crucial:

- Integration within the strategic institutional priorities championed by the college president
- Financial and human resource support for the effort

Philosophical and financial support provided the necessary lift to repurpose nineteen existing positions and hire eight additional advisors. In addition, the timeliness of a $2 million Department of Education Title III grant provided rapid, coordinated deployment of technology and reporting infrastructures to support the model.

Despite these assets, advising reform is complex and campus-specific. The importance of building community and gathering input from all stakeholders cannot be overstated. High-quality, responsive advising programs have the extraordinary potential to unify campus communities around the shared purpose of moving students toward their goals. As we consider our experience, we offer five observations:

1. *Prepare for advisor turnover*. Develop as much of your training program as possible in an online, self-guided format, but be sure to pair new hires with a seasoned advising mentor. Consider developing lead advisor positions to provide ongoing training and professional development.
2. *Technology is essential, but it can be messy*. Advisors must adopt technology and use it seamlessly. Customizing technology takes time, effort, and substantial energy. Rather than adding more technologies to the mix, conduct an assessment of existing student-success technologies and associated business processes, and leverage what you already have. Reduce the number of tools advisors and faculty use. Focus on high-quality integration of the tools that are most useful and effective.
3. *Everyone IS watching because they are invested*. As your advising reform takes shape, devote time and energy toward managing the expectations of advisors and campus stakeholders. High-profile inclusion of advising within the student success framework is ideal, but it may come with extremely high expectations for the advisor role. Case management guidelines that strike a balance between uniformity and creativity are crucial so that outcomes can be achieved.
4. *Advising isn't magical*. Find tactful ways to remind the campus that advisors cannot be held accountable for every student success or failure. Providing students with a co-pilot to navigate their experience is invaluable, but to truly be successful, academic advising cannot, and should not, be done in a vacuum. Two-way partnerships, especially with faculty, are a necessity, and those relationships need constant nurturing.

5. *Encourage bravery, and open hearts and ears.* Listening to students, advisors, faculty, and staff is essential. Showcase the nuts and bolts of advising and seek opportunities to collaborate. Empower advisors to share the complexity of advising and the importance of identifying financial, personal, and academic barriers to success. The work matters, and developing a deep, shared understanding of the student experience will give your advising program synergy that leads to success.

REFERENCES

Bailey, T. R., Jaggars, S., & Jenkins, D. (2015). *Redesigning America's community colleges: A clearer path to student success.* Cambridge, MA: Harvard University Press.

Dweck, C. S. (2006). *Mindset: The new psychology of success.* New York: Random House.

Completion by Design. (2016). Building guided pathways: Practical lessons from completion by design colleges. Retrieved from http://completionbydesign.org/

Crane, L. R. (2008). 2008 Fact Book. Retrieved from https://hip.harpercollege.edu/our-college/IR/Documents/Fact%20Book%202008-2009.pdf

Hoffhines, K. (2018). *Case study: Evaluation of a case management advising model* (Doctoral dissertation, Ferris State University). Retrieved from http://hdl.handle.net/2323/6283

Karp, M. M. (2011). Toward a new understanding of non-academic student support: Four mechanisms encouraging positive student outcomes in the community college. CCRC Working Paper No. 28, Assessment of Evidence Series. Columbia University Teachers College, Community College Research Center.

Karp, M. M. (2013). *Entering a program: Helping students make academic and career decisions.* New York: Columbia University, Community College Research Center.

Karp, M., & Bork, R. (2012). They never told me what to expect, so I didn't know what to do: Defining and clarifying the role of a community college student. CCRC Working Paper No. 47. Columbia University Teachers College, Community College Research Center.

O'Banion, T. (2013). *Academic advising: The key to student success.* Washington, DC: Community College Press.

Scott-Clayton, J. (2011). *The shapeless river: Does a lack of structure inhibit students' progress at community colleges?* New York: Columbia University, Community College Research Center.

SIX
Building Pathways to Student Success at the Community College of Baltimore County

The Role of Academic Advisement in Guided Pathways

Nicole Baird and Jennifer Kilbourne

The Community College of Baltimore County (CCBC), located in suburban Baltimore County, Maryland, is a nationally recognized leader in innovative learning strategies among the nation's top associate degree–producing institutions. Originally established in 1957, CCBC was created following the merger of three Baltimore County area community colleges and is now the region's largest provider of higher education and workforce development training in the Baltimore metropolitan area.

With three main campuses and three extension centers, CCBC serves more than 62,000 students and offers more than 200 degrees, credit certificates, and career-training licenses and certificates. CCBC's mission is to provide accessible, affordable, and high-quality education that prepares students for transfer and career success to strengthen the regional workforce and enrich the community.

CCBC is nationally known for acceleration in developmental education through the implementation of the Accelerated Learning Program (ALP) and Accelerated Math Program (AMP) as a framework for increasing student success and enabling students to achieve college credits more rapidly. These accelerated models permit concurrent paired enrollment of developmental education courses with a college-level course within the same discipline.

The college became an Achieving the Dream (ATD) college in 2009 and currently holds the designation as an ATD Leader College. ATD is a national reform network of colleges committed to serving as a "source of innovation; a platform for scaling effective practices and policies; a set of peers with whom to share knowledge; and an expert group to define the next phase of the reform agenda" (Achieving the Dream, 2019). As a result of the institution's partnership with ATD, a college-wide ATD steering committee, Student Success 102 (SS102), was formed and included key leaders from every department in the college.

In 2011, CCBC was awarded a $1.9 million US Department of Education Title III Strengthening Institutions Program (SIP) grant titled, "Building a Culture of Success: Increasing Persistence, Retention, and Graduation." In addition to supporting developmental education course reform and an integrated enrollment services model, the Title III project supported a comprehensive advising and intervention initiative focused on the creation of a comprehensive advising system to ensure students stay on track through expanded assessment, academic planning, early alert, and intervention and support services. During the five years of the grant, the Academic Advisement department staff, as well as other members of the college, participated in continuous professional development and training.

In 2015, the college launched a Pathways initiative. To integrate Pathways across the college, the Office of Instruction; Office of Enrollment and Student Services; and Planning, Research, and Evaluation (PRE) department combined efforts to implement Pathways from the point of admission to degree completion. This process was coordinated by a college-wide SS102 steering committee, faculty Pathway coordinators, and Pathway advisors. The implementation of Pathways led to an even deeper examination of academic advisement processes. Thus, components of the academic advising program were selected by the college as its primary focus for participation in ATD.

CONTEXT OF ADVISING AT CCBC

CCBC students are advised primarily by professional academic advisors in a centralized location. Depending on prior learning experiences, new students are advised by admissions counselors or academic advisors. Students with no prior college experience are frequently advised by an admissions counselor. The admissions counselor reviews the college's multiple measures options and determines if the student will need to take the placement test. Multiple measures options include standardized exam scores (such as SAT, ACT, or GED) or cumulative high school grade point average (2.50 is considered college-ready for English and a 3.00 is considered college-ready for math).

The college also has an articulation agreement with the local school district that exempts students from needing to take the placement test upon successful completion of identified public high school coursework. Students with prior college experiences, including advanced placement or international baccalaureate classes or military credentials, see an academic advisor. However, although there are recommended points when students should see an academic advisor, there is no requirement for new students to return for further advising following assessment. Subsequently, a two-semester educational plan is created for new students.

Furthermore, with a student-to-advisor ratio of nearly 700:1, it is challenging for advisors to provide outreach to students. Students are not assigned to specific advisors and may see several different advisors during the registration process. To provide consistent messaging to students, advisors share session notes via Banner Student Information System (SIS). Banner SIS houses all student records and registration information.

ORGANIZATION OF ACADEMIC ADVISEMENT

In 2007, CCBC leadership realigned the organizational structure of the college. This design is still in place today and includes a vice president of Enrollment and Student Services. The vice president reports directly to the president of the college and provides leadership to three deans—one each for Student Development, Enrollment Management, and College Life.

The dean of Student Development oversees Academic Advisement, Career Services, Disability Support Services, Testing and Assessment,

Student Services and Retention Initiatives, and TRIO programs for the college. The college offers a centralized academic advisement model that is led by a single director of Academic Advisement. The director oversees professional academic advisement operations for the entire college. Four assistant directors report to the director of Academic Advisement and manage operations at assigned campus locations.

There are twenty-three full-time professional advisors and approximately forty-six part-time professional advisors throughout the year. In addition to the part-time advisors, Academic Advisement Centers hire part-time schedule assistants during registration periods (April to August and November to January) to assist new and continuing students with registration.

COMPONENTS OF PATHWAYS AND ACADEMIC ADVISEMENT

Academic advisement touches many aspects of Pathways at CCBC. Academic advisors are active participants in college-wide steering committees and faculty Pathway work groups. The academic advisors provide both support to faculty coordinators and engage students in pathway activities. In particular, academic advisement plays a key role in the development of high-quality course sequences to be used by both full-time and part-time students that provide pertinent program information and stackable credential and credit accumulation milestone information. The Academic Advisement department also has a voting member on the General Education Review Board and Learning Outcomes Assessment Advisory Board at CCBC.

Implementation of Meta-Majors

The components of CCBC's Pathways initiative follow the American Association of Community College's Pathways Model (AACC Pathways Model, 2019). CCBC implemented five meta-majors, termed "Pathways," in fall 2015. The initial Pathways included Arts and Humanities; Behavioral and Social Sciences (including General Studies); Pre-Allied Health; Business, Law, and Justice; and Technology, Science, and Mathematics. Although these groupings appeared to work well with the college's structure, after reflection, input from Academic Advisement, and two years of data evaluation, it became increasingly important to restructure and include a dedicated Pathway for General Studies students.

A General Studies Pathway was created to facilitate support for these students who compose more than 50 percent of the college's enrollment. In addition, other meta-majors were realigned to include groupings that were important to build cohorts with similar goals (students seeking traditional transfer degree programs versus those seeking career degree programs). Therefore, in fall 2017, CCBC implemented six Pathways as follows: Arts; Business, Law and Education; General Studies; Humanities and Social Sciences; Science and Health Careers; and Technology, Engineering and Mathematics.

One simple but important aspect of CCBC's Pathways is how each is represented by a unique color. Students may forget the name of their Pathway but relate to their Pathway's color. For example, a Nursing major in the Science and Health Careers Pathway may simply state, "I belong to the green pathway." All promotional materials for each Pathway are color-coded, and the general Pathways logo incorporates all six colors (http://www.ccbcmd.edu/Programs-and-Courses/Degrees-and-Certificates/Pathways.asp).

Each Pathway is managed by a dedicated faculty coordinator. Each coordinator receives twelve hours reassigned time per academic year. Faculty coordinators have various tasks that include developing, promoting, and implementing cross-Pathway and Pathway-specific activities; collaborating with CCBC's Offices of Student Life and Academic Advisement; collecting and distributing Pathways-associated data; updating the CCBC Pathways website and social media pages; engaging faculty in Pathways activities; and soliciting input from students, faculty, and staff regarding Pathways at CCBC. The lead faculty coordinator and director of the Academic Advisement department actively participate in SS102 meetings, providing essential feedback to that body to propel Pathways efforts forward. Additionally, academic advisors work closely with faculty coordinators to promote Pathways to students.

Although all academic advisors serve as generalists, each advisor is assigned to one of six Pathways. In this role, academic advisors serve as Pathway "information specialists" and provide guidance to colleagues and students on program information, Pathway activities, and high-impact practice. Furthermore, academic advisors serve as Pathway "experts" and help cross-train colleagues in areas of study. Academic advisors connect with program faculty in the assigned Pathway to complete a program inventory to collect updated academic and career information that may be useful during student meetings.

Although the Academic Advisement department attempts to match students with academic advisors who specialize in that student's Pathway, this is not always possible during peak registration times. However, academic advisors are also involved in the planning and implementation of Pathways activities and share this information with students.

Course Tracks

Course tracks have been an important part of the Pathways initiative from its start. The original purpose of these tracks was to move students through similar coursework within a Pathway, thus creating a cohort-like feel and decreasing wasted credits. Unfortunately, there were many obstacles using the course tracks, most notably the lack of coherence with the college catalog and published semester sequences. In addition, course tracks were built for full-time students and were difficult for part-time students to use.

In rethinking this concept, CCBC's School of Technology, Art, and Design, in coordination with Academic Advisement, began to develop course sequences using a model from St. Petersburg Community College in Florida (St. Petersburg Recommended Academic Pathway, 2019). In these sequences, courses are listed in the order in which they should be taken, providing a guide in which students can register regardless of whether they choose to be full- or part-time students. In addition, the sequences include information on prerequisites, general education coursework, program requirements, and electives. Academic Advisement is in the process of reviewing all course sequences developed by academic departments to ensure they align with the college catalog. Updated course sequences will be available for student and academic advisor use in fall 2019.

Transfer Collaborations/Efforts

Student success is expressed most visibly when students graduate and transfer to a four-year institution with minimal barriers. The Office of Instruction and the Academic Advisement teams are working to build stronger transfer relationships with the top transfer institutions: Towson

University (TU), University of Maryland–University College, University of Maryland–Baltimore County, and University of Baltimore (UB). The SS102 Seamless Transfer subcommittee was formed to encourage faculty and staff partnerships, Pathway and transfer student support, articulation and advisement, and research and communication.

Initial efforts have been forged with TU to develop and expand 2+2 agreements (STEM emphasis), 3+1 agreements, pretransfer advising by TU for CCBC students, advising models that complement CCBC's Pathways initiative, data sharing with respect to student progress, and opportunities for CCBC students to participate in select TU activities to support transfer success. In addition, a CCBC/UB Transfer Workgroup has been developing processes to improve admissions, advising, and articulation efforts between these institutions. Top transfer majors of CCBC students to UB have been identified, and efforts to support seamless transfer through both articulation and Pathways are underway. CCBC and UB have shared professional development opportunities, and CCBC hosts UB advisor days on the CCBC campuses. These opportunities for improved communication and partnership with local four-year institutions are essential for seamless transfer initiatives.

Developmental Education Acceleration

Acceleration efforts at CCBC began over a decade ago with the development, growth, and institutionalization of the ALP. The launch of Pathways coincided with a renewed focus on integrating developmental English and reading. CCBC consolidated four developmental courses (two levels of English and two levels of reading) with a maximum of sixteen billable hours into two courses. The first, ACLT 052, is a five-billable-hour integrated reading and English course that prepares students for college-level English composition. The second, ACLT 053, is designed to be taken in an ALP context, allowing concurrent enrollment in English Composition 101, permitting developmental education students the opportunity to earn college credit in their first semester. These courses are designed to highlight complex academic texts with a student-focused pedagogy throughout. ACLT 052, which is designed for students with the highest level of need, has an integrated Pathway component with the goal of providing awareness of the variety of options CCBC offers.

As one of the first student touch points, the Academic Advisement department plays an essential role in fostering student registration in accelerated developmental English, reading, and mathematics offerings. This is an important step for many students as approximately 63 percent of first-time students require some form of academic remediation upon enrollment. In addition, Academic Advisement plays an important role in training faculty and staff about procedures and polices relative to the college's multiple options for placement, including ALEKS for math, Accuplacer for reading and English, grade point average for recent high school graduates, standardized exams (e.g., GED, SAT, or ACT), and high school coursework.

New-Student Orientation

Upon the implementation of Pathways at CCBC, Student Life and the Office of Instruction worked to expand the new-student orientation (NSO) to include faculty participation and a presentation highlighting Pathways. The Academic Advisement department plays a key role in marketing NSOs to new students. Although Student Life implements this important student-success initiative, students first meet with Academic Advisement. During this process, advisors encourage students to participate in orientation. This connection is an important mechanism to build participation at these events.

At the orientations, students are given time to engage with faculty members, representatives from Student Life, and student support services to increase student engagement and understanding of college life. Students who attended NSO sessions in the fall of 2016 demonstrated spring 2017 retention rates of 78.8 percent, a rate 13 percent higher than new students who did not attend an orientation. In addition, for the fall of 2016, students who attended both the NSO and one Pathway activity demonstrated 86.5 percent retention rates in spring 2017. The overall CCBC student retention rate in the same academic year was 63.4 percent. Although these numbers cannot demonstrate causation, they certainly suggest participation in NSO and Pathway activities may be critical to student-retention efforts.

NSO is not mandatory, yet these data suggest that participation in orientation is important. To expand access to these orientations, CCBC's assistant director of Student Life, First Year Experience, developed and implemented an online version of the NSO. A link to this version can be accessed on the Blackboard home page and is available to all students and faculty throughout the year.

Contextualized Academic Development Course Assignments

CCBC's first-year-experience course, Academic Development (ACDV), not only serves as an effective practice, but also infuses connections to career and transfer, the primary outcomes of CCBC's Pathways initiative. ACDV is a one-credit, mandatory course for all new-to-college students and differs from NSO with respect to content. The career assignment in ACDV was modified, allowing students to examine career opportunities more deeply within the context of a selected Pathway. In addition, ACDV students present career posters at Pathways-sponsored Career Events in the fall and spring semesters. Academic advisors provide training and support for ACDV instructors who provide advising to new students, including the development of a DegreeWorks Educational Plan and explanation of policies, procedures, and curriculum requirements.

Blackboard Organizations

CCBC uses Blackboard as a learning management system (LMS). Blackboard includes shells that can be populated by students and staff outside a course section termed "organizations." Students are connected to their Pathway via these Blackboard organizations. Organizations serve both to host resources for students, such as information on Student Success Centers, Academic Advisement, and internships, and as an effective communication tool for each Pathway. Students are automatically enrolled based on the majors they select.

Pathway Activities

One major kick-off event, called Connectfest, engages students in Pathways, student organizations, and student support services across the college. Faculty and academic advisors from each Pathway engage students in conversations about career and college goals and encourage students to participate in pathway activities for the coming academic year. Student Life presents students with opportunities for cocurricular learning, including leadership development and civic engagement offerings along with campus-based student organizations.

Additionally, these events serve to connect students to vital resources such as Academic Advisement, College and Community Outreach, the library, the Writing and Literacy Center, Continuing Education, and the

Student Success Center (tutoring). In fall 2018, over 1,450 CCBC students participated in ConnectFest programs at the three main campuses and one extension center. These events provided important connections for students outside the classroom, and is evolving into a major student engagement activity at the college.

Faculty pathway coordinators, academic advisors, and members of Pathway committees organize cocurricular, Pathway-specific activities such as field trips; transfer and advising sessions; career sessions; test preparation workshops; and Pathway-specific lectures, discussion groups, and performances. These activities are intended to fully immerse students in their field of study and career interests. In 2017–2018, just over 5,000 students attended Pathway activities.

General Studies Mentoring Project

In fall of 2017, CCBC reorganized the Pathways to include a dedicated Pathway for General Studies students. In fall of 2018, a mentoring program was piloted for those students with the following goals:

- Provide support and encouragement as students move through CCBC.
- Foster goals of retention and degree completion and help students acclimate to the culture of higher education.
- Help students identify their academic and career objectives.
- Assist students in moving to the academic pathway best suited to their goals.

Faculty were chosen through an application process and provided training from Student Support Services colleagues, including academic advisors. During the fall 2018, thirty-five faculty members participated, and seventy-five General Studies students were mentored. Academic Advisement's role in the training of faculty mentors was essential to provide consistent and timely information to students.

PROFESSIONAL DEVELOPMENT FOR ACADEMIC ADVISORS

Ongoing training and professional development are necessary and crucial components of any high-quality, comprehensive academic advisement program. Also crucial is the assessment of the advising program and individual advisors and recognition and rewards for those who deliver academic advising (Gordon, Habley, & Grites, 2008). Comprehensive advisor training and development should be an intentional, ongoing process.

Training and development should be focused on the specific needs of all who provide advisement. Thus it is vital that training materials be accessible and up to date. Hence, Academic Advisement leadership created a Blackboard course that houses electronic copies of training materials, college policies and procedures, and examples of best practices. New academic advisors (full time or part time) are assigned a mentor. The mentor is typically a seasoned academic advisor who will orient the mentee to the college and monitor training. In addition, new advisors complete training modules within the LMS that contain quizzes to measure academic advisor's mastery of the content. The Blackboard training site is available to faculty advisors, General Studies faculty mentors, and other staff across the college.

Additionally, Academic Advisement subcommittees were formed to target specific topics and develop a robust training program. To further support ongoing professional development, all full-time academic advisors are required to attend at least three Innovative Educators webinars each year. Innovative Educators is an online product that offers live and on-demand webinars to professionals in higher education. The webinars focus on a variety of areas that include customer service, retention strategies, athletic advisement, online advisement, and other topics. Upon completion of the webinar, academic advisors are required to report what they learned and discuss how any new strategies can be used.

SPECIAL FEATURES OF CCBC'S ACADEMIC ADVISEMENT MODEL

As the institution continued to refine the Pathways model, it became clear that a case-management approach would be helpful to some special populations. The college understands that it takes a village to guide and foster student growth. Beginning in fall 2017, two case-management pilot programs were designed and implemented to support student journeys on CCBC's Pathways: athletic advisement and embedded advisors in developmental education courses.

Athletic Advisement

Academic Advisement incorporates a holistic, case-management advising process for student-athletes. Full-time, professional academic advisors participated in specialized training to advise student athletes. Following this training, each advisor was assigned to campus-specific athletic teams and served as a liaison for academics, student development, and athletic departments. The assigned advisor met with each student-athlete a minimum of three times a semester (preferably once a month) to check on academic progress and connect students with appropriate resources, as applicable. In addition, advisors provided career and transfer exploration and educational planning. The advisors taught special sections of ACDV 101 for new student-athletes, hosted study skills and informational workshops, marketed Pathways opportunities, and attended athletic events. This allowed advisors to not only build a stronger relationship with the student but with the athletic coaches as well.

Embedded Advisors in Developmental Education Courses

CCBC's Academic Advisement team is composed of many part-time advisors. Traditionally, part-time advisors' hours are reduced during nonpeak enrollment periods because of the decline in student visits and as a budgetary savings. However, this approach made it challenging to retain staff and keep everyone up to date on changes in policies and procedures. Thus there was a need to implement a pilot designed for the students who most needed proactive intervention while building a student caseload for a highly trained part-time workforce. Hence, the Advisors Promoting Proactive Learning Experiences (APPLE) pilot emerged.

The APPLE pilot was a college-wide initiative that partnered the Academic Advisement department with the Instruction department for the purpose of promoting and supporting student success, retention, and completion. After reviewing success rates in developmental courses, Academic Literacy (ACLT) was selected for the pilot. The ACLT 052 course is a five-billable-hour, integrated reading and writing course. This course serves as a prerequisite for college-level English composition (ENGL 101) for students who did not demonstrate college readiness in reading or sentence skills on the placement test or via other assessment options.

Part-time advisors were selected through an application process and awarded a guaranteed minimum number of hours to work per week;

their hours were not reduced once the peak registration period ended. Each part-time advisor was also assigned a full-time advisor mentor and was assigned one section of ACLT 052, a one-semester, fourteen-week course, to provide outreach and case management to enrolled students.

Using a similar approach to the athletic advisement advisors, the part-time advisor's objective was to build a partnership with the ACLT 052 faculty member and students by:

- Conducting one-on-one meetings with students outside of class throughout the semester (at least twice) and making at least two classroom presentations
- Providing regular "walk-in" office hours to connect with students outside of class and refer students to college resources
- Following up on faculty progress reports regarding student absenteeism, lateness, missing assignments, failed quizzes and tests, and behavioral concerns with the student
- Assisting the student with registration for the subsequent semesters
- Continuing to provide case management to the students as they move forward into subsequent semesters

After a year of offering the APPLE program, it is still under evaluation. However, data indicate that students enrolled in APPLE sections were retained at a slightly higher rate than students in non-APPLE sections. Although the data did not demonstrate higher final course grades in APPLE versus non-APPLE student sections, faculty and academic advisors enjoyed the partnership and the collaborative approach toward student success. Additionally, students seemed to have a deeper connection to the academic advisor.

Technology

CCBC uses the Banner Student Information System. Academic advisors use Banner daily to access student records and to record case notes. Academic advisors also use DegreeWorks to complete educational plans for all students. However, academic advisors frequently refer to a host of other web-based resources to counsel students on transfer options, study skills, career exploration, and other areas students may need.

Over the last two years, the use of technology to communicate with students has grown in response to a growing online course offering. Following the emergence of CCBC Online, one of the college's newest initiatives supporting more than twenty online programs, Academic Advisement needed to discover and implement creative ways to advise students virtually. Hence, academic advisors advise students via video conferencing, phone, or email. The college is also using text messaging as a tool to connect with students. In fact, text messaging is a tool used by APPLE advisors and athletic advisors to communicate with students on their caseload. The college is currently piloting a new chat tool to help guide students though general questions about the college.

FUNDING

In addition to institutional operational funds, dedicated budgets for each of the Pathways provides funding for part-time advisors. These funds support academic advisors' attendance to Pathways-related functions and professional development. Although the budget for each Pathway is minimal, it does provide dedicated resources to support Pathway activities throughout the academic year.

PROGRAM EVALUATION

The college has a long history of making data-informed decisions with respect to the identification of goals, implementation of strategies to enact progress toward goals, and for use of data and metrics to assess progress of those goals. Since the inception of Pathways, CCBC has collected data to assess the effects of these efforts and measure student progress. The college's PRE office, working with the SS102 Steering Committee, Academic Advisement, and Pathway faculty coordinators, provided support for data analysis by developing reports to identify students by Pathway and program major for targeted outreach, reviewed employee survey feedback for insights and attitudes about Pathways, analyzed transfer outcomes using methods recommended in CCRC guides, and analyzed outcomes for students participating in Pathways events between fall 2016 and spring 2018.

Preliminary data demonstrate that students who attended Pathways activities took more courses with higher success rates in those courses, were more likely to end the semester in good academic standing, and had significantly higher next-semester retention rates than students who did not attend Pathways events. These preliminary results are encouraging and worthy of further study.

SUMMARY

The CCBC Pathways initiative has been successful in providing efficiency and creativity in breaking down silos across the college to build and implement important student success initiatives. This has already led to some important collaborations, and an enduring structure is in place for future work. This work is helping the whole institution begin to come together around a single vision of an effective student experience at the college, from outreach in the high schools through successful completion of a degree or certification, all while exploring career and transfer options. CCBC's work on Pathways has been defined by constant effort, consistent refinement, and the need for this work to be performed at scale. A large institution such as CCBC reaps immense benefits for work in Pathways.

However, at an institution as large as CCBC, the benefits of scale come with some drawbacks. For all the work accomplished in strengthening Pathways, most students do not feel a connection to their Pathway. Although a lot of information was collected from the Academic Advisement pilot programs that are currently in place, this has not translated into a holistic experience for every student. Students need a person. Students need a consistent person at the institution to serve in the role of mentor, guide, advisor, and liaison. Thus the institution is in the initial stages of identifying best practices in the development of assigned academic advisor to take this work to the next level.

An assigned advisor, either professional advisor or faculty, allows students to build relationships with someone outside of the classroom to foster students' journeys to their goals using a case-management approach. Furthermore, whether the student's goal is to transfer to a four-year institution or pursue a workforce credential, the information provided to the student is consistent and relevant. Coupled with the need to establish and expand case-management efforts is the need for technology to track and communicate student's progress. Thus the institution is currently researching options to identify technology that would provide a platform for this level of intervention.

As an institution, the first four years of work on the Pathways system have created a strong foundation for future success. The first step was to create motivation for change and reform in the system that can be used to fully align CCBC with the best practices of the Pathways model. The next steps are to integrate these pieces into a coherent and holistic experience for each student. Pathways will continue to be an evolving process that will require continuous examination and evaluation. Hence, there is much work left to do.

REFERENCES

Achieving the Dream. (2019). *Our network.* Retrieved from https://www.achievingthedream.org/our-network?section=netstat

American Association of Community Colleges. (2019). AACC Pathways Project. Retrieved from https://www.aacc.nche.edu/programs/aacc-pathways-project/

V. N. Gordon, W. R. Habley, & T. J. Grites (Eds.). (2008). *Academic advising: A comprehensive handbook (2nd ed.).* San Francisco, CA: Jossey-Bass.

St. Petersburg Community College. (2019). Recommended Academic Pathway-Business Administration. Retrieved from https://info.spcollege.edu/Community/AP/_layouts/15/WopiFrame.aspx?sourcedoc=/Community/AP/Shared%20Documents/Current_BUS_AS.xl

SEVEN

Establishing a Culture of Completion through Advising at West Kentucky Community College

Renea Akin and Octavia Lawrence

West Kentucky Community and Technical College (WKCTC) is one of sixteen colleges that comprise the Kentucky Community and Technical College System (KCTCS). Located in the bend of the Ohio River in Paducah, Kentucky, the college enrolls 8,200 students annually. The institution's history dates to 1909 when one parent institution, West Kentucky Technical College, was established as West Kentucky Industrial College, a teacher training college for African Americans. The other parent institution, Paducah Community College, was founded in 1932 as Paducah Junior College. The two institutions consolidated in 2003 to become West Kentucky Community and Technical College.

 A comprehensive community college, WKCTC is committed to providing high-quality educational experiences, meeting the educational needs of the college community, serving as a full partner in business and workforce development, and contributing to the overall economic and social well-being of the region. The college offers two-year transfer Associate in Arts, Associate in Science, and Associate in Fine Arts degrees; and Associate in Applied Science degrees, diplomas, and certificates that lead to direct entry into the job market. WKCTC was recognized by the Aspen Institute as one of the top ten community colleges in the nation in 2013 and 2017 and was recognized as a Finalist with Distinction in 2011 and 2015.

EVOLUTION OF ADVISING AT WKCTC

From the beginning, WKCTC made a commitment to offer an academic advising program that actively supports teaching and learning. To better serve its students, WKCTC moved all student services to a single location to enable new and returning students to enroll at the college, complete placement testing (if needed), meet with an advisor and financial aid counselor, register for classes, pay fees, and purchase books in a single location.

WKCTC participated in the John Gardner Institute Foundations of Excellence Transfer and First Year Experience project in 2011. As a result of engaging in this review, WKCTC established a Central Advising Council (CAC) charged with facilitating dialogue regarding the college's advising processes and sharing advising information between and among faculty and staff. The CAC serves as the advisory board for general academic advising processes including promotion of transfer opportunities. Poch (2017, p. 191) notes, "Accurate information communicated effectively to and from various units, brings together those concerned with first-year students' academic and personal welfare."

Regular advising meetings and participation in advising groups keeps advisors apprised of changes in policy or procedures. Each academic division is represented on CAC. Faculty representatives are charged with collecting important advising information and disseminating it to the members of their respective divisions.

Also as a result of participating in the John Gardner Foundations of Excellence program, in 2014 WKCTC began offering an optional three-credit-hour, first-year experience course, FYE 105 Achieving Academic Success. Because community college students arrive with "limited understanding of the opportunities and demands of college life and lack the skills and orientation needed to thrive in a college culture" (Zeidenberg, Jenkins, & Calcagno, 2007, p. 6), early intervention is required for a culture of completion to thrive. Student-success courses offered early in the students' academic career are effective practices that promote student engagement, academic and career mapping, and timely credential completion (Greenfield, Keup, & Gardner, 2013).

First-year experience courses provide an opportunity for students to acclimate to the college environment, learn how to navigate the institution, develop academic skills and study habits, and establish academic and career goals (Cho & Karp, 2013). These courses also encourage students to explore personal strengths and aptitudes and align their strengths with specific careers or college majors (Stovall, 2000).

The purpose of the WKCTC FYE 105 course is to introduce students to strategies that promote academic, personal, and professional success in the college environment; foster a sense of belonging; promote engagement in the curricular and cocurricular life of the college; and provide opportunities for students to develop academic plans that align with career and life goals (*KCTCS Catalog*, 2018).

To address credit-hour limits in technical programs, in 2015, the college developed two one-credit-hour FYE courses, FYE 1051 Orientation to College and FYE 1053 Academic, Financial and Personal Skills, to allow students in certain majors to benefit from a first-year experience course without accumulating excessive credit hours. A review of preliminary retention data led the faculty to recognize the value of FYE 105 in facilitating student success. Ultimately, the faculty elected to require completion of FYE 105 by new credential-seeking students effective fall 2016.

Also, in 2016, in light of upcoming state implementation of performance-based funding, the college conducted an internal review to identify areas of focus to further enhance and support student success. Academic advising and career pathways emerged as key, and intertwined, areas to support student persistence and ultimately completion. Supporting a culture of completion is crucially important not only for the institution, but also for students because students' ability to secure financial aid increasingly depends on steady progress toward a degree (Fox & Martin, 2017). Recognizing that academic advising is an effective practice that can directly affect retention and completion (Darling, 2015), the college once again focused its attention on improving its academic advising processes, specifically advising processes for first-year students.

Although first-year experience courses have long been noted as effective tools for acclimating students to the college environment, standalone courses do not "embrace a comprehensive, holistic (whole-person) approach to promoting student success" (Cuseo, n.d., p. 1). Designing first-year experiences in collaboration with other institutional priorities such as advising promotes partnerships that contribute to "a more integrated first-year experience" (Cuseo, n.d., p. 4) and have been found to be most effective when tied to other campus initiatives (Natalicio & Smith, 2005). After reviewing the literature and consulting with experts in the field, WKCTC embedded specific academic advising improvements in FYE 105 that blend advising and career pathways and led to the creation of a learning-centered, student-focused advising protocol, *Chart Your Own Course!*

To facilitate alignment of WKCTC first-year student experiences, the college adopted the use of a visual tool to track student progress toward credential completion. Visual tools help unify advising efforts and provide clear benchmarks leading to completion. Visual tools also illustrate information students receive in the first year and provide a guided pathway to navigate the student's college experience. The WKCTC *Chart Your Own Course!* visual tool illustrated in figure 7.1 includes a navigational map that outlines the steps a student takes to completion, beginning with the application process and ending with graduation.

By integrating advising into a first-year experience course, *Chart Your Own Course!* actively engages students and advisors in "the cocreation of clear and intentional education plans that lead to completion of goals and future success in education, careers, and the workplace" (Darling, 2015, p. 87). Because the first year of college is "the most crucial advising period for both advisors and students" (Damminger & Rakes, 2017, p. 23), embedding active advising into the first-year experience course is crucial in establishing a culture of completion.

ORGANIZATIONAL STRUCTURE

The National Academic Advising Association (NACADA) identifies academic advising as the core of student success (NACADA, 2017). The WKCTC academic advising model is multifaceted and aims to provide advising services that support the teaching and learning process and assist students in meeting their academic and career goals. Academic advising at WKCTC is shared by academic affairs and student services.

The Advising Center is staffed with four full-time professional advisors, one enrollment specialist, one accessibilities specialist, and one administrative assistant. Each professional advisor has a caseload of advisees of approximately 125 students. In an effort to provide more comprehensive and effective services to students, the Advising Center serves as

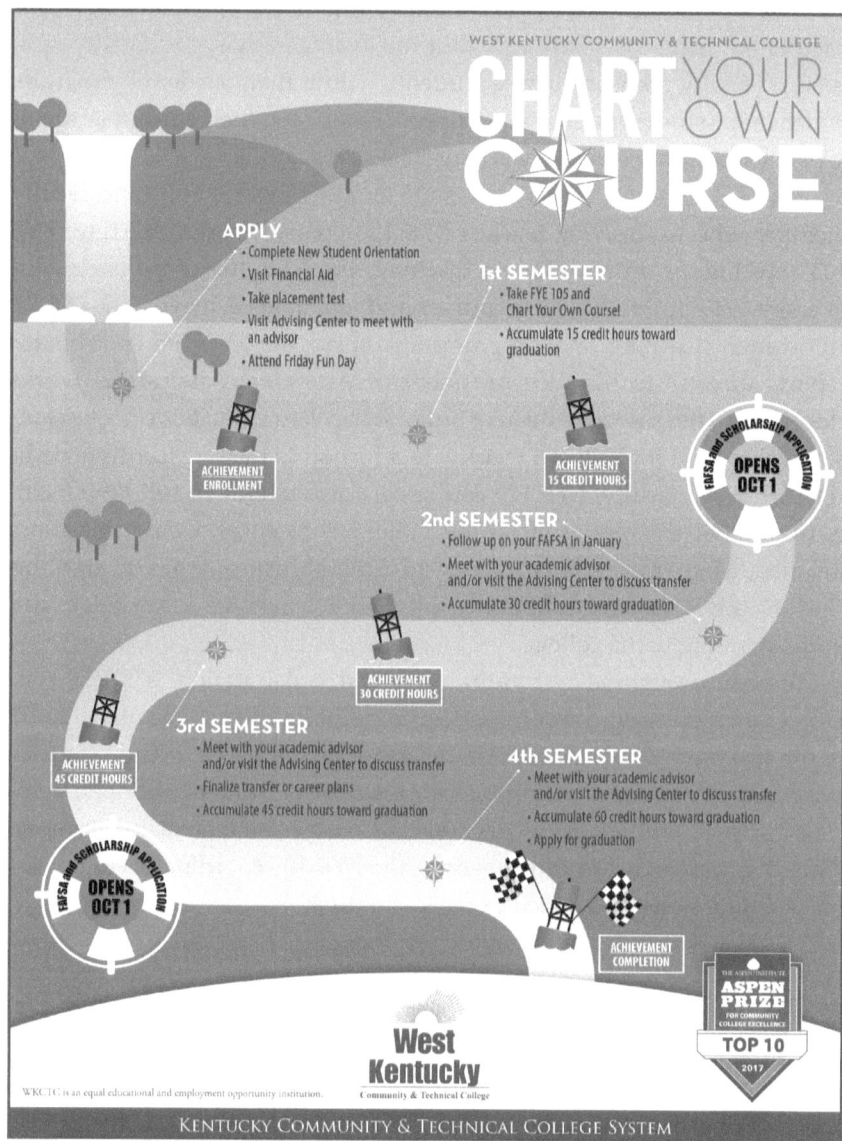

Figure 7.1. Steps to Completion

the point of entry for new, transfer, veterans, accessibility, and online students. Although one advisor serves as the lead for each area, all professional advisors are cross-trained and equipped to work with all student populations.

WKCTC also employs approximately one hundred faculty advisors. Faculty advising caseloads vary, but the average advisee to faculty ratio is 50:1. Faculty advisors advise students within their academic program, which helps students make the connection between their current academic plans and future career goals (Cuseo, n.d., para. 47).

WKCTC first-year experience staff includes both a full-time faculty member who exclusively teaches FYE 105 courses, and a full-time FYE 105 coordinator. In addition to teaching, the FYE 105 coordinator also oversees scheduling FYE 105 courses and evaluates achievement of FYE 105 student learning and program outcomes. The FYE 105 coordinator reports directly to the vice president of Academic Affairs and works closely with the associate dean of Student Services to facilitate professional development for FYE 105 faculty. In addition to the two full-time dedicated FYE 105 faculty, FYE 105 courses are also taught by full-time faculty from other disciplines including Biological Sciences, Communication, Reading, Mathematics, Business, and Criminal Justice; WKCTC staff, including advisors; and adjunct faculty with extensive knowledge and understanding of the college.

To ensure ongoing communication and collaboration, a *Chart Your Own Course!* steering committee meets monthly to review the progression of the program. The members of the steering committee include the vice president of Academic Affairs, vice president of Student Services, associate dean of Student Services, associate vice president of Institutional Planning, Research and Effectiveness, the FYE 105 coordinator, the director of Admissions, and a faculty representative.

COMPONENTS OF *CHART YOUR OWN COURSE!*

Advising community college students presents challenges because commuter students often lack engagement with faculty, staff, and other students, which can leave students feeling marginalized (Kodama, 2002). In addition, academic advising in the two-year college setting is challenging because of the heterogeneity of the student body, the variety and complexity of decisions students must make, and the frequent need for developmental programs of study to prepare students for collegiate work. WKCTC strives to meet the needs of its student body, which varies widely in academic potential and academic interest.

The mission of the WKCTC Advising Center is to provide accessible, innovative, and comprehensive advising services within an environment of excellence and commitment to student success. The Advising Center accomplishes its mission by providing and coordinating undergraduate and transfer advising services, providing professional development to faculty advisors, coordinating student placement and assessment services, monitoring student progression, and providing students with services to facilitate transfer and entry into the job market.

The WKCTC Advising Center's philosophy reflects the overall purpose of the academic advising program and is guided by the Developmental and Appreciative Advising models. To support a culture of completion, it is imperative that the advisor and advisee collaborate and invest in a relationship that supports completion and growth. The academic advising structure at WKCTC reflects the shared structure and the supplementary model created by C. F. Pardee (2004).

Appreciative advising is the "intentional, collaborative practice of asking positive open-ended questions that help students optimize their educational experience and achieve their dreams, goals, and potentials" (Appreciative Advising, n.d.). Appreciative advising aims to "identify personal strengths and sources of motivation to heighten individual potential through positive questioning" (Hutson, 2010, p. 4). Through the six phases of this model (Disarm, Discover, Dream, Design, Deliver, and Don't Settle), the advisor helps the student recognize strengths and interests, clarify goals, and guides the student in creating strategies to achieve those goals in a timely manner.

Developmental academic advising "is the use of interactive teaching, counseling, and administrative strategies to assist students to achieve specific learning, developmental, career, and life goals. These goals are set by students in partnership with advisors and are used to guide all interactions between advisor and student" (Creamer & Creamer, 1994, p. 19). The developmental advising model strongly influences the advising student learning outcomes at WKCTC. Developmental advising is a "systematic process based on a close student-advisor relationship intended to aid students in achieving educational, career, and personal goals through the utilization of the full range of institutional and community resources" (Winston, Miller, Ender, & Grites, 1984, p. 8).

Four student learning outcomes were developed to reinforce the advising philosophy at WKCTC. Students are expected to:

1. Formulate and clarify goals related to academic and career choices.
2. Demonstrate knowledge of academic requirements.
3. Develop a tentative course schedule prior to advising sessions.
4. Use campus resources as needed.

Each learning outcome is designed to help students recognize the skills needed to successfully navigate their academic and career goals. Achievement of the learning outcomes requires a strong partnership and understanding between the academic advisor and the student.

FYE 105 instructors serve as the academic advisor for their respective first-time FYE 105 students. This model provides FYE 105 instructors an opportunity to develop interpersonal relationships with their students, engage in multiple conversations about their interests and plans, clarify academic and career goals, and help the students develop academic plans to completion. Incorporating appreciative advising into FYE 105 further complements and enhances the FYE 105 instructor's advising role.

As noted previously, although the majority of FYE 105 courses are staffed with full-time WKCTC faculty, some sections are taught by adjuncts or nonadvising staff such as the director of Financial Aid. Because of the criticality of advising to student success, students seeking an Associate in Arts or Associate in Science degree enrolled in FYE 105 sections taught by adjuncts and nonadvising staff are assigned to professional advisors in the Advising Center. These professional advisors serve as the students' advisor until graduation. FYE 105 students seeking an Associate in Applied Science degree enrolled in sections taught by adjuncts and nonadvising staff are assigned to faculty advisors in their respective major their first semester. The faculty member serves as the students' advisor until graduation. The decision tree that illustrates this process is provided in figure 7.2.

Recognizing the need to tailor advising to individual needs, students not already assigned a permanent advisor are assigned to an advisor during their second semester. Advisors are assigned to students in a systematic process based on academic preparedness and program plan. Undecided students are assigned to the professional advisors in the Advising Center. Students who qualify for TRIO Student Support Services are assigned to TRIO advisors. All others are assigned to faculty advisors based on major or program plan of study. This system pairs students with advisors who are experts in particular areas through background experience, personal interest, or professional development.

Establishing a Culture of Completion

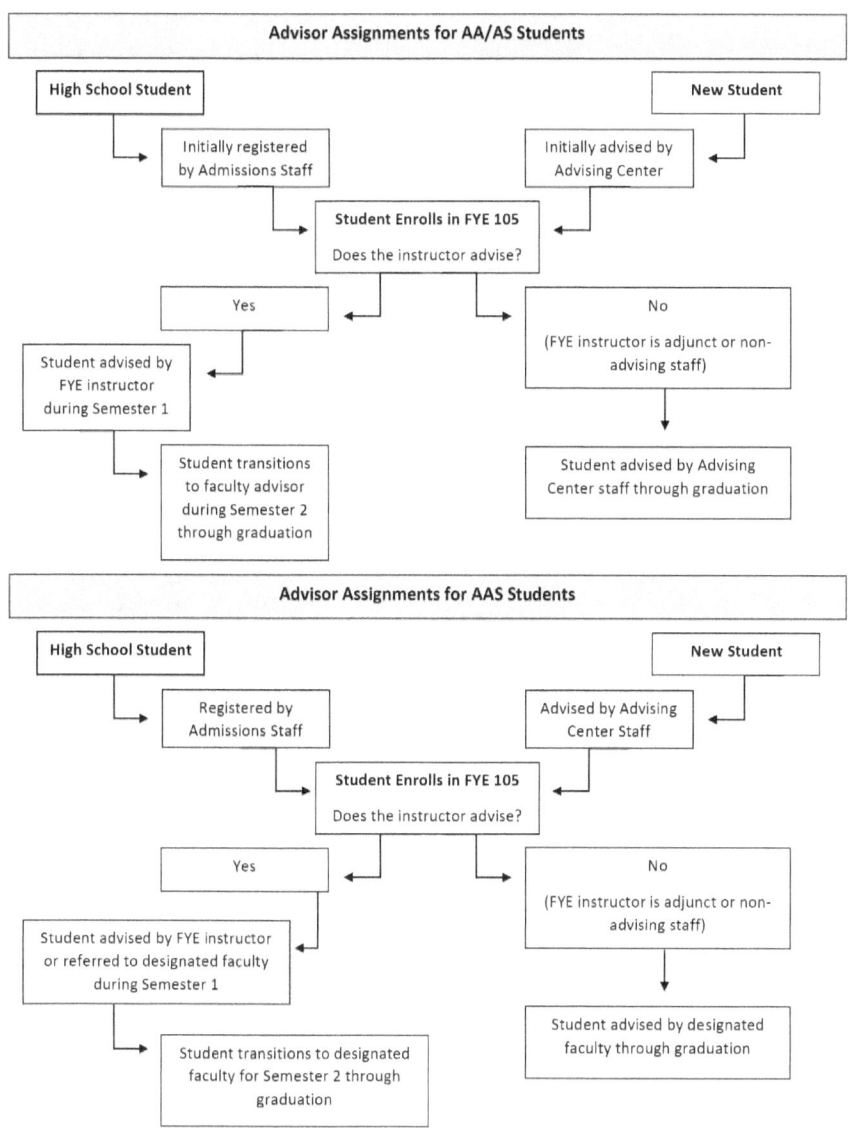

Figure 7.2. FYE 105 Decision Tree

The bulk of academic advising at WKCTC is a joint effort between Advising Center staff and full-time faculty. Advising is an important component of faculty responsibilities. Academic advisors are "uniquely positioned to address these issues as they view the holistic undergradu-

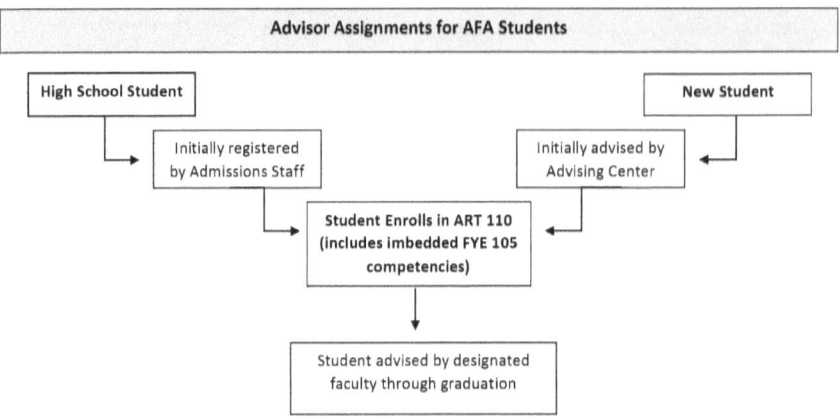

Figure 7.2. FYE 105 Decision Tree (continued)

ate experience from the perspective of the student and create success plans that address concerns and educational goals" (Darling, 2015, p. 88).

The quality and effectiveness of faculty advising activities are considered for progress toward promotion and tenure and factor into the annual performance review for all full-time faculty members. Faculty fulfill their academic advising obligations by working directly with assigned advisees and by working with unassigned advisees in the Advising Center for a set number of hours each academic year. Staffing the Center with teaching faculty ensures students have ongoing contact with experienced faculty advisors throughout the year. Faculty report to an academic dean; the academic deans report to the vice president of Academic Affairs.

Collaboration and communication are key components of the college's advising program. Effective partnerships between Academic Affairs and Student Services have enabled the college to be creative and flexible in developing an academic advising program that integrates multiple campus resources to meet students' educational needs.

StrengthsFinder

Two crucial elements that tie advising to the first-year experience curricula and ultimately enable students to chart their own course include the StrengthsFinder and Career Pathway FYE 105 assignments. The StrengthsFinder assignment requires students to identify characteristics about themselves and match those characteristics to an appropriate career choice. The Clifton StrengthsFinder is a web-based personality assessment developed from the perspective of the field of positive psychology (Gallup CliftonStrengths, 2018). The StrengthsFinder measures the presence of talents in thirty-four general areas, referred to as *themes*. According to Gallup, talents are the foundation of strengths development because they are naturally occurring thoughts, feeling, and behaviors (Gallup CliftonStrengths, 2018). Upon completion of the assessment, students receive a report detailing their top five most dominant themes.

WKCTC piloted the StrengthsFinder in spring 2016. After students identified their strengths, the director of Career Services led classroom discussions designed to help students understand how to identify potential careers that capitalize on their strengths. Based on positive feedback from students and FYE 105 faculty, the StrengthsFinder was adopted in all FYE 105 sections in fall 2016.

In fall 2016, FYE 105 instructors completed the StengthsFinder and developed a student assignment and grading rubric. The assignment required students to complete the StrengthsFinder and write a short reflection addressing the following questions:

- What are your top five strengths?
- Do any results surprise you? Why or why not?
- What are some common misconceptions about your strengths? How can you positively address these?
- Which strength will most help you in achieving academic success? Why?
- In what ways do these strengths align, or not align, with your career interests?

A meeting in May 2017 with FYE 105 instructors revealed the need to further revise the StrengthsFinder portion of the course to emphasize the need for students to capitalize on their personal strengths when identifying a potential career. A revised FYE 105 StrengthsFinder assignment was launched in fall 2017. The revised assignment requires completion of a formal written report that focuses on in-depth analysis of personal strengths and career pathways instead of a short reflection. The assignment is assessed using a grading rubric that assesses each of the following elements of the revised assignment:

- Part One: Top Five Strengths

- In your own words, define your top five strengths.
- Part Two: Domain Analysis
  - Identify the domains where your top five strengths reside.
  - What does this reflect about you and experiences? Provide an example of a time or experience that demonstrates your prominent domains.
- Part Three: Academic and Career Alignment
  - Identify your intended career choice.
  - Explain how your top five strengths and the prominent domains align with your academic and career goals. Be specific in how you believe *each* of your strengths will apply in your future career.

To standardize the use of the grading rubric, the FYE 105 coordinator collects StrengthsFinder assignments from all FYE 105 sections each fall and facilitates a grade norming session each spring. Following the session, faculty participate in activities to address any identified grading inconsistencies. Standardizing use of the StrengthsFinder rubric helps students identify a career goal that appropriately aligns with personal strengths. Incorporating an intentional assessment of student strengths into FYE 105 supports Tinto's (2016, p. 3) assertion that colleges must "see to it that students enroll in a field of study appropriate to their needs and interests." In fall 2017, 460 of the 522 students (88 percent) who completed this assignment met the student learning outcome that students will identify a career goals that aligns with individual strengths.

Career Pathway

FYE 105 students identify academic and career goals, design an academic plan to accomplish their goals, and identify college resources and student support services designed to help overcome challenges to academic success. Students complete a capstone assignment, the Career Pathway, which ties together the following FYE 105 student learning outcomes:

1. Develop an educational plan that leads to a career path.
2. Research and understand career choices.
3. Research and understand transfer options.

4. Locate and use campus resources.
5. Demonstrate use of information technology.
6. Develop self-management skills.
7. Develop strategies for academic success.

The Career Pathway project requires students to map their timelines to credential completion from the first semester to the last. To successfully complete the project, students must pay particular attention to selective admission requirements, financial aid implications, developmental course work, personal factors that may influence time to completion, and resources needed to reach their career goal.

On an annual basis, the FYE 105 coordinator collects learning outcomes for the course; learning outcomes are assessed using the Career Pathway assignment rubric. This grading rubric was created when the college began offering FYE 105 and is refined each year as the Career Pathway evolves. To standardize the use of the Career Pathway grading rubric, the FYE 105 coordinator also facilitates a grade norming session for the Career Pathway assignment each semester. Following the session, faculty meet to address grading inconsistencies. Standardizing use of the Career Pathway rubric helps students strengthen their understanding of their academic and career pathways. In fall 2017, 432 of the 521 students (83 percent) who completed this assignment met the student learning outcome that students will develop an academic plan that aligns with the identified career goal.

In addition to increased use of academic and student support services, the percent of students responding "Quite a bit" or "Very much" to the CCSSE survey item that asks, "How much has your experience at this college contributed to your knowledge, skills and personal development in developing clearer career goals?" increased from 62 percent in 2014 to 70.7 percent in 2018. The college will obtain additional qualitative feedback from students pertaining to their development of career goals through biannual focus group analysis.

Aligning advising with structured activities in FYE 105 enables students to chart their own course by aligning academics and student support services with shared practices and resources that empower students to take ownership of their academic and career goals. Aligning campus practices and resources to enhance the students' ability to navigate college, explore career goals, and pursue academic plans to reach their career goals establishes a culture of completion.

PROFESSIONAL DEVELOPMENT

According to Damminger and Rakes (2017, p. 19), "Effective advisors build trusting relationships with advisees, which they leverage when co-constructing road maps for an educational journey that culminates in a degree or credential." To maximize the effectiveness of advisors, WKCTC invests heavily in faculty and staff professional development. All new faculty and staff participate in a year-long First-Year Information (FYI) orientation program. This program consists of shared faculty and staff experiences and includes a full-day orientation followed by monthly meetings designed to build camaraderie and provide focused training on specific areas of the college. In addition, all new faculty participate in additional orientation activities, including an overview of advising that provides faculty with the basic skills needed to advise students.

Because the advising needs of students in different academic programs vary, new faculty are assigned mentors within their academic division and spend time "shadowing" experienced faculty advisors. This allows the new faculty advisor to become better acquainted with the specific advising needs of the students in the academic area in which they teach.

For example, although all faculty advisors are able to use the published curriculum guides to advise students in an allied health or nursing academic program, a faculty advisor who teaches in this area will be able to share personal experiences in the clinical setting with students to help them decide if they are pursuing the appropriate career path. The mentoring program enables experienced faculty to share this type of knowledge, which is difficult to quantify. All faculty advisors annually participate in required professional development provided by Advising Center staff to alert faculty to any changes in the advising process.

As part of *Chart Your Own Course!* WKCTC identified and implemented best practices to create and support a culture of completion, including the development of a comprehensive professional development plan. Research on advising models prompted the adoption of the "appreciative advising" model, which is designed to foster interpersonal relationships that build social and academic engagement to enhance the student's overall educational experience and promote timely credential completion.

Advising at WKCTC is a shared responsibility between the Advising Center staff and full-time faculty. Each semester before the enrollment period begins, pertinent advising information is disseminated through the CAC for faculty and staff to use and inform their advising sessions with students. The adoption of the appreciative advising model complements the CAC and further assists students in the timely achievement of their academic and career goals. The University of North Carolina at Greensboro successfully integrated the appreciative advising model into their first-year experience course and found growth in "student wellness, their sense of belonging and acceptance, and their self-perception of interdependence" (Hutson, 2010, p. 11). In addition, term GPA and next-year retention were higher for students in the cohort compared with students in the comparison group (Hutson, 2010).

The professional development needed to implement appreciative advising is achieved through the advising partnership, which consists of cohorts of faculty and staff who undergo year-long training in the use of the appreciative advising model. Providing professional development to cohorts builds a support mechanism for participants. Structured time "devoted to sharing advising knowledge turns out to be perhaps most critical for professional development and practice" (Poch, 2017, p. 192).

Participants begin their professional development with a half-day Appreciative Advising Institute and attend three appreciative advising workshops per semester led by the WKCTC associate dean of Student Services. The first advising partnership cohort included FYE 105 faculty, advising center staff, and representatives from departments such as TRIO Student Support Services and Admissions. Membership in subsequent advising partnership cohorts consists primarily of faculty advisors.

Faculty and staff participants have responded positively to the advising partnership as evidenced by reflections from cohort participants such as, "The advising partnership provided several opportunities that strengthened my skills. First, the chance to get together with other advisors in our monthly meetings and focus on each stage of appreciate advising allowed me to gather ideas, to reflect on my own approach in each stage, and to feel less alone in the gigantic responsibility of serving as an advisor."

Other advising partnership participants noted, "This partnership helped me to have some dedicated time to focus on my advising. Often, because of my large advising load, I simply begin to go through the motions, in particular during the last month of the semester. This partnership provided some structure to understand the role of advising and for what makes excellent advising. It also strengthened my resolve to handle each advisee as unique opportunities to help students to change their world." In addition, one participant mentioned that the advising partnership created a space for her to "understand the advisee more now than previously."

Coordinated efforts between Academic Affairs and the Advising Center create an environment that values academic advising professional development. Professional development is provided through the CAC, the advising partnership, and by faculty and professional advisors. A faculty resource guide is created and maintained by the Advising Center staff and serves as a handbook for faculty advisors. The Advising Center serves as a resource for advising at WKCTC.

TECHNOLOGY

Technology is a key element in the advising process at WKCTC. Through the years, advising technology has evolved and helped support the academic advising program at WKCTC. The research on the effectiveness of advising technologies is limited, but preliminary evidence indicates "such reforms can have a positive impact on student outcomes, particularly when the technology-mediated intervention or alert is coupled with an additional person-to-person interaction" (Kalamkarian, Karp, & Ganga, 2017).

A student-management system, early alert system, interactive academic plans, and comprehensive advising notes support effective advising on campus. Faculty and staff advisors use the student management system to assist students. Advising technology allows advisors to track graduation requirements, evaluate student process, enroll students, and document important advising interactions.

Updated transfer plans and interactive academic plans help advisors and students better understand course requirements. The ability to upload academic plans to the student advising record strengthens advising consistency and the students' experience within advising. Technology helps to engage the student in academic planning. Austin (Texas) Community College reported that students who used their course planning tool were "2.4 percentage points more likely to persist over the course of three terms compared with students who did not use the tool" (Kalamkarian, Karp, & Ganga, 2017).

FINANCIAL SUPPORT

After careful review of the fiscal requirements needed to develop a culture of completion, WKCTC is committed to fiscally supporting the advising program. The *Chart Your Own Course!* budget was approved by the WKCTC leadership team in 2017. The budget includes funding for personnel, professional development, and operational expenditures. The personnel category includes the salary and benefits of two full-time faculty (FYE 105 coordinator and FYE 105 faculty) and overload pay for full-time faculty and staff teaching FYE 105. The total cost to implement *Chart Your Own Course!* over five years is approximately $1 million.

PROGRAM EVALUATION

A comprehensive assessment plan measures the effects of *Chart Your Own Course!* The assessment plan includes both direct assessment of student learning through in-class assessment and indirect assessment through the use of institutional measures. The assessment plan also includes a qualitative analysis to support the quantitative findings. Assessment is the responsibility of the *Chart Your Own Course!* steering committee which meets regularly to evaluate progress toward reaching the program's five-year targets. The FYE Program Coordinator creates an annual report that is shared with WKCTC constituencies.

In addition to the two student learning outcomes previously mentioned, *Chart Your Own Course!* includes a student learning outcome that students will demonstrate continued, measurable progress in the timely completion of academic goals. WKCTC tracks fall-to-spring and fall-to-fall retention, three-year graduation rates, and three-year transfer rates for FYE 105 enrollees compared with first-time students who do not take FYE 105. As illustrated in figures 7.3 and 7.4, fall-to-spring and fall-to-fall retention rates are higher for students taking FYE 105 compared with other first-time students not taking FYE 105.

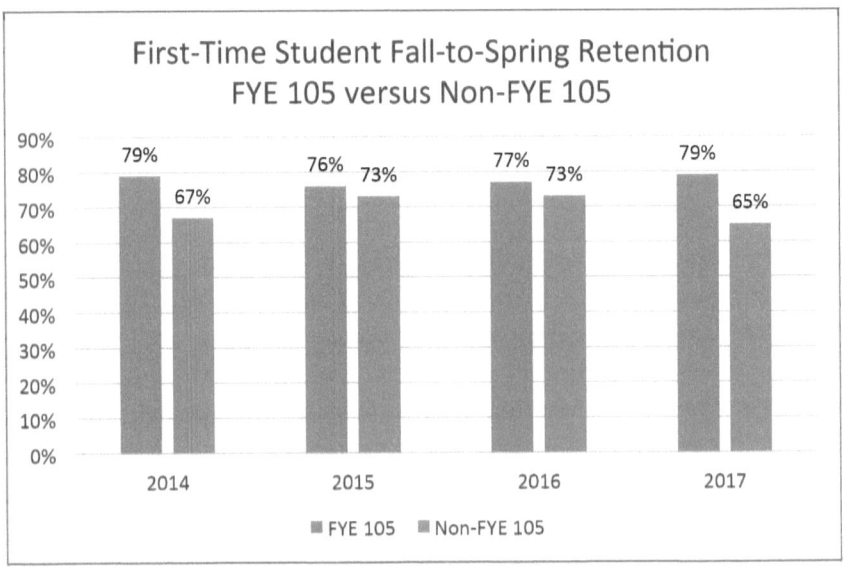

Figure 7.3. Fall-to-Spring Retention Rates

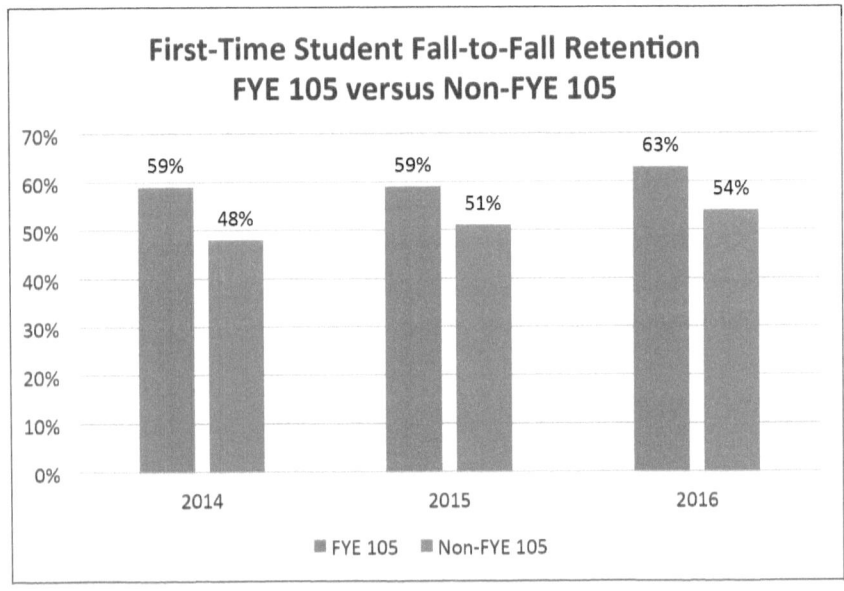

Figure 7.4. Fall-to-Fall Retention Rates

Graduation and transfer rates are evaluated at the end of three years for each cohort. Table 7.1, FYE 105 Three-Year Graduation and Transfer Rates, illustrates graduation and transfer rates for the 2014 and 2015 cohorts. Even though the WKCTC graduation rates for the 2014 and 2015 cohorts include both full- and part-time students, graduation rates still exceed the 150 percent of normal-time graduation rate of 23.6 percent for first-time, full-time degree or certificate-seeking students at two-year public postsecondary institutions (U. S. Department of Education, National Center for Education Statistics, 2018).

Table 7.1. FYE 105 Three-Year Graduation and Transfer Rates

	2014 Cohort	2015 Cohort
Graduation Rate	39.5%	38.1%
Transfer Rate	18.1%	16.7%

A PERSONAL PERSPECTIVE

From 2002 to the present, academic advising at WKCTC has evolved from a culture of schedule building to a culture of providing comprehensive advising services grounded in teaching and learning that foster personal growth and a sense of responsibility for academic and career goals. The *Chart Your Own Course!* program at WKCTC unites academic advising with a first-year experience course to support a culture of completion by aligning academics and student support services with shared practices and resources that empower students to take ownership of their academic and career goals. *Chart Your Own Course!* was developed with the student in mind and is based on scholarly research and best practices. The program is succeeding because it is a true collaborative effort between academic affairs and student services. Faculty and staff engage in robust professional development activities designed to foster a culture of completion. Ongoing success of this initiative depends on continued cooperation between academic affairs and student services.

Other institutions wishing to launch their own version of *Chart Your Own Course!* should take the time to thoroughly review existing support structures to allow for the integration, rather than the creation, of systems and supports to provide students with an integrated first-year experience that tie together existing campus resources.

The WKCTC academic advising model empowers students to become responsible for their own academic success. Advisors are committed to providing accurate and comprehensive academic advising. Working together, students and advisors develop one-on-one relationships and share responsibility to assist students to make choices and define goals, guide students through administrative processes, develop meaningful educational plans, connect students to campus services and resources, and encourage the intellectual growth of students.

REFERENCES

Appreciative Advising. (n.d.). What is appreciative advising? Retrieved from https://www.appreciativeadvising.net/about-us.html

Cho, S., & Karp, M. (2013). Student success courses in the community college: Early enrollment and educational outcomes. *Community College Review*, 86–103.

Creamer, D. G., & Creamer, E. G. (1994). Practicing developmental advising: Theoretical contexts and functional applications. *NACADA Journal 14*(2), 17–24.

Cuseo, J. (n.d.). Empirical case for the positive impact of the first-year seminar—Research on student outcomes. Paper presented at the 31st Annual Conference on the First-Year Experience, San Antonio, Texas, 2012.

Darling, R. A. (2015). Creating an institutional academic advising culture that supports commuter student success. *New Directions for Student Services, 150,* 87–96. doi: 10/1002/ss

Damminger, J., & Rakes, M. (2017). The role of the academic advisor in the first year. In J. R. Fox & H. E. Martin (Eds.), *Academic advising and the first college year* (pp. 181–198). Columbia, SC: University of South Carolina, National Resource Center for the First-Year Experience and Students in Transition and NACADA: The Global Community for Academic Advising.

Fox, J. R., & Martin, H. E. (Eds.). (2017). *Academic advising and the first college year* (pp. 181–198). Columbia, SC: University of South Carolina, National Resource Center for the First-Year Experience and Students in Transition and NACADA: The Global Community for Academic Advising.

Gallup CliftonStrengths for Students. (2018). Retrieved from https://www.strengthsquest.com/help/general/143093/personality-theory-cliftonstrengths-assessment-based.aspx

Greenfield, G. M., Keup, J. R., & Gardner, J. N. (2013). *Developing and sustaining successful first-year programs: A guide for practitioners.* San Francisco, CA: Jossey-Bass.

Hutson, B. L. (2010). The impact of an appreciative advising–based university studies course on college student first-year experience. *Journal of Applied Research in Higher Education, 2*(1), 3–13.

Kalamkarian, H. S., Karp, M. M., & Ganga, E. (2017). *Advising redesign as a foundation for transformative change.* New York: Columbia University, Teachers College, Community College Research Center.

Kentucky Community and Technical College System. (2018). *KCTCS Catalog 2018–2019.*

Kodama, C. M. (2002). Marginality of transfer commuter students. *NASPA Journal, 39*(3), 233–250.

NACADA: *The Global Community for Academic Advising.* (2017). Retrieved from https://www.nacada.ksu.edu/

Natalicio, D., & Smith, M. (2005). Building the foundation for first-year student success in public, urban universities: A case study. *Challenging and Supporting the First-Year Student,* 155–175.

Pardee, C. F. (2004). Organizational structures for advising. Retrieved from the *NACADA Clearinghouse of Academic Advising Resources* http://www.nacada.ksu.edu/Resources/Clearinghouse/View-Articles/Organizational-Models-for-Advising.aspx

Poch, S. (2017). Advisors' Tools, Resources, and Partnerships. In J. R. Fox & H. E. Martin (Eds.), *Academic advising and the first college year* (pp. 181–198). Columbia, SC: University of South Carolina, National Resource Center for the First-Year Experience and Students in Transition and NACADA: The Global Community for Academic Advising.

Stovall, M. (2000). Using success courses for promoting persistence and completion. *New Directions for Community Colleges, 112,* 45–54.

Tinto, V. (2016, September 26). How to improve student persistence and completion. *Inside Higher Ed.* Retrieved from https://www.insidehighered.com/views/2016/09/26/how-improve-student-persistence-and-completion-essay

U.S. Department of Education, National Center for Education Statistics. (2018). The condition of education 2018 (NCES 2018-144), Undergraduate Retention and Graduation Rates.

Winston, R., Miller, T., Ender, S., & Grites, T. (1984). *Developmental academic advising.* San Francisco: Jossey-Bass.

Zeidenberg, M., Jenkins, D., & Calcagno, J. C. (2007). *Do student success courses actually help community college students succeed?* (CCRC Brief No. 36). New York: Community College Research Center, Teachers College, Columbia University.

About the Contributors

Courtney Adkins is the assistant director of publications at the Center for Community College Student Engagement at the University of Texas at Austin. She has been with the Center for over fifteen years. In her current role, she provides guidance to the Survey Operations team and manages all publications and website content. Before coming to the Center, Courtney taught English full time at Baton Rouge (Louisiana) Community College. She has also taught as an adjunct faculty member at several institutions. Courtney holds a PhD in English from the University of Louisiana at Lafayette.

Renea Akin is the associate vice president of Institutional Planning, Research, and Effectiveness at West Kentucky Community and Technical College in Paducah, Kentucky. Her work focuses primarily on planning, assessment, and accreditation. She is a graduate of the University of Kentucky, University of Indianapolis, and Vanderbilt University.

Vicki Atkinson is the dean of Student Development and an associate professor at Harper College in Palatine, Illinois. Vicki's scholarship focuses on first-year and new-student transition issues in community colleges. As a licensed professional counselor, Vicki combines her research interests in student success and completion with intrusive advising and counseling techniques. In addition, Vicki is an advocate of action research as a method to support the training and professional development of community college professionals. Vicki is a graduate of Northern Illinois University with an EdD in Adult and Higher Education.

Nicole Baird is the dean of Student Development at the Community College of Baltimore County (CCBC). She oversees Academic Advisement, Student Services and Retention Initiatives, four federal-grant-funded TRIO programs, Career Services, Disability Support Services, and the Testing Centers. With over eighteen years of administrative experience supporting community college students, she held several progressive roles as the director of Testing and Assessment, the director of Developmental Education, coordinator of the Student Success Center, and Supplemental Instruction Coordinator. Additionally, she taught developmental math as well as first-year experience courses as an adjunct faculty member. Baird also served as the president of the Developmental Education Association of Maryland. Because of her commitment to researching and implementing best practices in education, she is committed to developing programs that foster the success of community college students. She is a graduate of Coppin State University and is currently enrolled at Drexel University in pursuit of a Doctorate in Educational Leadership and Management.

Elisabeth Barnett, senior research scholar at the Community College Research Center at Teachers College, Columbia University, also serves as associate director of the National Center for Education, Schools and Teaching at Teachers College. Barnett's research interests relate to access to college, the high school–college transition, dual enrollment, student assessment, workforce education, and student supports. She has written numerous articles and reports and is viewed as a nationally recognized expert on college readiness. Barnett received her PhD from the University of Illinois at Urbana–Champaign in Educational Organization and Leadership with a focus on higher education.

John Britt is the director of Advising at Valencia College, Osceola Campus. His career within student affairs began at the University of Central Florida in 2009 where he mentored student athletes who competed in baseball and basketball. From 2011 until the present, he has served Valencia College as an academic advisor, atlas lab coordinator, interim dean of students, and most recently campus director of advising. He has contributed to the implementation of a new proactive advising model at Valencia providing assigned advising to students based on their intended program of study. Additionally, he cofacilitates Valencia's PIVOT 360 leadership program. John is a graduate of Florida State University and the University of Central Florida.

Ed Holmes is the director of Advising at Valencia College, West Campus. He began his position in 2013 thanks to a Department of Education Title III Grant; he led the redesign of advising at his college, establishing a proactive advising model that provides major-specific academic pathways for students as well as career and academic advising embedded within a credit-bearing course (New Student Experience). Holmes was deeply involved in Valencia's implementation of its Quality Enhancement Plan (QEP), which was the primary catalyst for establishing New Student Experience faculty in the professor-advisor duel role. Ed has been at Valencia since 2001 and is a graduate of the University of Central Florida.

Hoori Santikian Kalamkarian is a senior research associate at the Community College Research Center at Teachers College, Columbia University. She conducts research on system-wide and statewide reform efforts, including the implementation of technology-based advising systems and redesign of developmental education. Kalamkarian holds a bachelor of arts in English and political science from the University of California–Los Angeles and a PhD in education from Stanford University.

Jennifer Kilbourne is the assistant dean of Curriculum and Assessment in the Office of Instruction at the Community College of Baltimore County, a large, multicampus institution in Maryland. Her work focuses on general education outcomes assessment, student learning outcomes assessment, high-impact practice infusion models, program review, and program development. She has worked on the implementation of guided pathways since their inception at CCBC and currently serves as a member of the Student Success steering committee that oversees this initiative. She is a graduate of Salisbury University and the George Washington University.

Serena Klempin is a Research Associate at the Community College Research Center at Teachers College, Columbia University, where she conducts qualitative research on advising and student supports. She is also a doctoral student in the Sociology and Education program at Teachers College, Columbia University. Her dissertation examines the role of higher education in addressing students' basic needs. She holds a bachelor of arts from Kenyon College and the master of social work from the Columbia University School of Social Work.

Octavia Lawrence is the associate dean of Student Services at West Kentucky Community and Technical College in Paducah, Kentucky. Previously, she served as the director of Advising at West Kentucky Community and Technical College. Her work focuses on advisor professional development, advising initiatives, and partnering with faculty and staff to improve advising practices. She is a graduate of Fisk University and Western Kentucky University.

Evelyn Lora-Santos began her career in higher education at Long Island University where she served as the director of Career Services. She also worked at the University of Central Florida where she served as the assistant director of Graduate Career Services. She joined Valencia College in 2013 as director of Advising on the East Campus where she oversees new-student orientation, advising, and career services. Lora-Santos has led the redesign of a proactive advising model and the implementation of a competency-based advisor training program. She has taught first-year experience and career development for sixteen years, and she is deeply involved in initiatives that strengthen academic and student affairs partnerships. She is a graduate from Pace University and Hunter College.

Sheryl Otto is associate provost for Student Affairs at William Rainey Harper College. During her more than thirty years in higher education she has provided leadership on a variety of initiatives, including advising redesign, early alert, transfer articulation, outcomes assessment, program review, student information systems implementation, and retention-based programming. She serves on the steering committee for the Illinois Articulation Initiative, is a former NASPA IV–East Regional Board member, and has presented at numerous local and national conferences. Otto holds a bachelor of arts in Communication from the University of Michigan and a master of arts in College Student Personnel from Bowling Green State University.

Lauren Pellegrino conducts qualitative research for projects related to the implementation and evaluation of Integrated Planning and Advising for Student Success, and guided pathways reforms at the Community College Research Center (CCRC). Lauren earned a PhD in educational research and policy analysis with a concentration in community colleges at North Carolina State University. She holds a bachelor and a master of business administration from Stetson University in Florida. Prior to joining CCRC, Lauren worked as a business administration instructor and quality enhancement plan assessment team member at Wake Technical Community College in Raleigh, North Carolina.

Kathleen Plinske serves as executive vice president and provost at Valencia College in Orlando, Florida. Prior to joining Valencia in 2010, Plinske began her career at McHenry County College in Illinois. Plinske earned a bachelor of arts in Spanish and Physics from Indiana University, a master of arts in Spanish from Roosevelt University, a doctorate in Education from Pepperdine University, and a master of business administration from the University of Florida. Deeply committed to increasing access to higher education for underserved populations and closing equity gaps, she was selected as an Aspen Presidential Fellow for Community College Excellence.

Evelyn Waiwaiole is the executive director of the Center for Community College Student Engagement at the University of Texas at Austin. Evelyn has spent seventeen years at the university in various roles, including serving as the Suanne Davis Roueche National Institute for Staff and Organizational Development Director and project manager of various grant-funded projects. Her work focuses on ensuring that the student voice is a part of the institutional improvement process. She earned a doctorate from the University of Texas at Austin in higher education administration, with a specialization in community college leadership; a master's in economics from the University of Oklahoma; and a bachelor's in psychology from Texas A&M University.

About the Editor

President emeritus of the League for Innovation in the Community College and senior professor of practice, Kansas State University, **Terry U. O'Banion** has worked in the field of community colleges for fifty-nine years. He has consulted at more than one thousand community colleges and authored seventeen books and over two hundred articles on the community college. Five national awards have been established in his name, including the Microsoft Student Champion Award and the Educational Testing Service O'Banion Prize for Teaching and Learning. He has been a dean at two Florida community colleges; vice chancellor of academic affairs at the Dallas County Community College District; a professor of higher education at Illinois, Berkeley, Texas, Toronto, Hawaii, and NOVA; and president of the League for Innovation in the Community College for twenty-three years. O'Banion earned a bachelor of arts in English (with honors), a master's degree in counseling from the University of Florida, and a PhD in higher education administration from Florida State University.

www.ingramcontent.com/pod-product-compliance
Lightning Source LLC
Chambersburg PA
CBHW022015300426
44117CB00005B/199